THE WORLD'S GREATEST
ALIEN CONSPIRACY
THEORIES

Photograph Acknowledgements

Fortean Picture Library 10, 13, 14, 16, 21, 46, 48, 72, 76, 99, 113, 115, 120, 143/Peter Brookesmith 7/Michael Buhler 138/Loren Coleman 81/Peter Jordan 78, 82, 83/Gary Marshall 144/Peregrine Mendoza 23

THE WORLD'S GREATEST
ALIEN CONSPIRACY THEORIES

Nigel Cawthorne

CHANCELLOR
PRESS

This edition published by Chancellor Press,
an imprint of Bounty Books, a division of
Octopus Publishing Group Ltd,
2-4 Heron Quays, London, E14 4JP

Printed in 2002

ISBN 0 7537 0565 6

Printed and bound in Great Britain by
Mackays of Chatham

Contents

1 This Alien is Deceased

The Roswell Incident

The most famous UFO encounter in history occurred on 2 July 1947. On that day, a flying saucer crashed near Roswell in a remote part of New Mexico. News reached the newspapers on 8 July. But having proof positive that aliens were visiting Earth so scared the American authorities that, later that day, they denied it had ever happened. This was the start of a UFO cover-up that exists in every country in the world to this day.

Crashed saucer display in UFO Enigma Museum, Roswell, New Mexico, USA.

The headline of the *Roswell Daily Record* of 8 July 1947 could not be clearer. 'RAAF Captures Flying Saucer on Ranch in Roswell,' it said in sixty-point type. Other newspapers carried equally unambiguous headlines: 'Army Finds Air Saucer in New Mexico' and 'Army Declares Flying Disc Found' were two of them. And they were not making it up. The story came from the horse's mouth – the Army itself. News of the UFO crash at Roswell was given to the world in press release issued by Lieutenant Walter Haut, Press Officer at the Roswell Army Air Field (RAAF). UFOlogists, with some justification, say that this was the most important press release of the twentieth century.

When it came to the cover-up, the timing of the press release proved crucial. It was issued at noon Mountain Time. This meant that it was too late for most morning papers. However, it did just catch some evening editions on the West Coast. Newspapers called the base at Roswell to check out the story. They were happy to expand on the press release. The sheriff's office and local newspapers were also inundated with queries. Then suddenly, without any warning, the Air Force killed the story. They said that what they had found was not a UFO after all. It was just a weather balloon.

The headlines the next day effectively buried the story: 'Reports of Flying Saucers Dwindle; New Mexico "Disc" is only Weather Balloon.' Local papers carried pictures of the wreckage. And that was the end of it.

Over thirty years later nuclear physicist and UFOlogist Stanton Friedman went to a TV station in Louisiana for an interview about his UFO work. Before he went on, Friedman was chatting with the station manager, who told him that he ought to go and talk to a man named Jesse Marcel who lived nearby in Houna, Louisiana. Marcel, the station manager said, 'handled pieces of one of those flying saucers you're interested in when he was in the military'.

The next day, Friedman tracked down Marcel and discovered that he had been the intelligence officer at the RAAF. He told Friedman that sometime after World War II a flying saucer was supposed to have crashed near Corona, New Mexico, just seventy-five miles north-west of Roswell. Marcel had been ordered to collect the crash wreckage and deliver it to Wright Field in Dayton, Ohio, where the US Army stockpiled captured enemy equipment. Marcel was on his way to Ohio, when Haut issued his press release. But later that day, when the brass in Washington heard about the incident, it was decided to hush everything up and a second statement was issued to the press, this time saying that the wreckage was that of a weather balloon.

Unfortunately, Marcel could not remember exactly when this had happened, but Friedman and fellow UFOlogist William Moore began an investigation. They got lucky. British TV personality Hughie Green had been in Pennsylvania at the time and had heard a report of the downed UFO on the radio. Though he never discovered any more, his story was carried in the very first edition of *Flying Saucer Review*. Green's account narrowed the date of the crash down to late June or early July 1947.

Moore trawled through the newspaper archive of the library of the University of Minnesota Library and found editions from 8 July 1947 covering the Corona–Roswell event. The papers gave the name of the rancher who owned the land where the crash had occurred, the local sheriff and the RAAF personnel involved. By 1980, Friedman and Moore had interviewed sixty-two people involved with the event, including neighbours who had also handled some debris – such as Loretta Proctor, and Jesse Marcel's son, Jesse junior – and Bill Brazel, son of the rancher who found the wreckage. Amazingly, Walter Haut, the Press Officer who released the story, still lived in Roswell. He had a copy of the base yearbook and was helpful in tracking down people and filling in details. And he was adamant that the debris he had seen at Roswell Army Air Force base was not the wreckage of a weather balloon.

'Anyone with any experience in the Air Force would be able to tell you the difference between a weather balloon and a flying disc,' he said. 'I'd seen them go up over the base – you'd look at them and say: "It's a weather balloon." A balloon is a balloon is a balloon.'

His boss Colonel Blanchard must have been convinced too. He authorised Haut to issue the press release.

The story of the Roswell crash began on the night of 1 July 1947. There was a thunderstorm that night over the small town of Corona, seventy-five miles north-west of Roswell. In the middle of it, there was a huge explosion. The following morning, Mac Brazel, a sheep farmer who operated the Foster Ranch twenty miles south-east of the town, went out to check on a water pump. On his way, he discovered an area over half-a-mile long strewn with debris. The pieces he picked up were made of a material he had never come across before. When he folded it several times, it spontaneously unfolded. There were also pieces of I-beam, which was as light as balsa wood but could not be broken or bent. Inside the 'I' of the beam, there were unusual symbols in a lavender-coloured pigment.

Brazel did not know what to do with the wreckage, so on Sunday, 6 July, he made the long cross-country trip to Roswell with some of the debris in the back of his pickup truck. He took it to the office of Roswell Sheriff George Wilcox. Wilcox, in turn, called the Army Air Force base. He was put through to the intelligence officer Major Marcel. When Marcel checked out the material, he

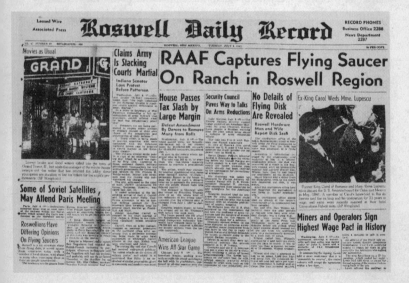

Front page of the *Roswell Daily Record*, 8 July 1947.

concluded that it was unlike any debris seen during his service in World War II. And Marcel was experienced in these matters. He was the intelligence officer for the world's then one and only atomic-bomb unit. Roswell was home to the 509th Bomb Group, which, in 1945, had tested the first atomic bomb at the nearby White Sands Missile Range.

Marcel reported the find to Roswell base commander, Colonel William Blanchard. He instructed Marcel and counter-intelligence officer Sheridan W. Cavitt to go back to the ranch with Brazel and collect the rest of the debris.

'When we arrived at the crash site, it was amazing to see the vast amount of area it covered,' Marcel said. 'It was nothing that hit the ground or exploded on the ground. It's something that must have exploded above ground, travelling perhaps at a high rate of speed... It was quite obvious to me, familiar with air activities, that it was not a weather balloon, nor was it a plane or a missile.'

The two officers collected as much debris as their vehicles could hold, but they had to leave a lot of it behind when they set off back to Roswell. On the way back to the base, Marcel could not resist stopping off at his home to show the wreckage to his wife and their son, Jesse junior.

'My father was so excited about the debris that he drove by our house to show my mother and me the material before delivering it to the air base,' says Jesse Marcel Jr. 'There were several boxes of it in our car but we emptied the contents of just one of these boxes on our kitchen floor. He wanted to see if he could piece some of the fragments back together.'

According to Jesse Jr., the debris contained a lot of metal foil. It looked like aluminium, although its surface was not so reflective.

'I didn't try to bend it,' he says, 'nor did I witness the "metal with a memory" that some have described. I do recall my dad saying a colleague had tried to bend one of the larger pieces with a sledgehammer without denting it.'

Jesse Jr. said that the most striking parts of the material were the beams.

'The one I remember best was about twelve to eighteen inches and was made from a very lightweight material. When I held it up to the light I could see what appeared to be symbols printed or embossed along the length of the beam,' he says. 'They looked at first like hieroglyphics, but on closer scrutiny appeared to be geometric designs.'

The next morning, Colonel Blanchard had the Corona crash site sealed off. The military police and a large body of soldiers were sent to the Foster ranch. They were making a detailed search of the area when, back at the Army Air Force base, press officer Lieutenant Haut issued the famous press release. The news appeared in the evening editions of the local papers and was quickly picked up by the radio stations.

By this time, Major Jesse Marcel and the wreckage were on board a B-29 on their way to Wright Field (which is now known as Wright–Patterson Air Force Base) in Ohio. On the way, they stopped at Fort Worth, Texas, headquarters of the Eighth Air Force.

By this time, General Clemens McMullen, the Acting Director of Strategic Air Command (SAC) in Washington, had heard about the press release and taken immediate action. He contacted the Chief of Staff at Fort Worth, Colonel Thomas Jefferson DuBose, and told him to invent a cover story. Given the sensitive nature of the incident, base commander General Roger M. Ramey was put in charge.

Colonel DuBose later explained why the cover-up was put into action. 'We had just gone through a World War, then came this flying saucer business,' he said. 'It was just too much for the public to have to deal with.'

When Marcel touched down at Fort Worth, he was met by General Ramey. 'Don't say anything,' Ramey ordered. 'I'll take care of it.'

The weather-balloon cover story had already been dreamed up. The base's meteorologist Irving Newton provided some home-made wreckage – a mangled radar reflector made of foil and a few wooden sticks. Marcel posed by the 'wreckage' and the press was told that a mistake had been made. What had crashed to Earth in New Mexico was not a flying saucer, but a radar reflector. After the photo-call, Major Marcel was sent back to Roswell where he was forbidden to speak to anyone. When he returned home, he told his wife and son not to talk about the crash to anyone, either strangers or friends.

The cover story hit the newswires at about 5 p.m. Central Time. It was too late for the newspapers, except the last edition of the *Los Angeles Herald Express,* which added to their flying saucer story the subheading: 'General Believes it is Radar Weather Gadget.'

When Lieutenant Haut heard about the cover-up he was appalled, but there was nothing he could do.

'A balloon may have crashed, but it certainly had nothing to do with the downed saucer,' he says. 'What most people don't realise is that, back then, you didn't ask questions – you did whatever your superior told you. Today, there'd be a lot of questions, or even a Congressional hearing, but it was a different era then.'

The military moved in on the Foster ranch. After two days, the main body of the saucer was found not far from the ranch house. The search for debris was then expanded and, just over a mile from the craft, the bodies of two dead aliens were found. Over the following week, the military cleared up the debris and surrounding area.

Not all the debris may have found its way to a top-secret cache. On 24 March 1996, a visitor marched into Roswell's International UFO Museum and handed over a fragment of metal which he said he had got from a retired serviceman who had been involved in the clean-up of the

Major Jesse Marcel, intelligence officer at Roswell Army Air Field in July 1947, holds the tattered remains of a flying disk found on a sheep ranch seventy-five miles from Roswell.

crash debris. Under police escort, it was taken to the New Mexico Bureau of Mines and Mineral Resources where it was examined by metallurgist Chris McKee. X-ray fluorescence analysis showed that the fragment was 69 per cent silver and 31 per cent copper, and McKee concluded: 'There was nothing associated with it to suggest an exotic origin.' The fragment is still under investigation and remains under police protection.

Friedman and Moore published six papers about the crash at Roswell and, eventually, in 1986, Friedman persuaded the producers of NBC's *Unsolved Mysteries* to do a segment about Roswell in their TV show. By this time Friedman and Moore had tracked down ninety-two people involved in the case, but in his role as a consultant to the production he continued investigating the case. It was then that he got to the bottom of a mystery that had been bugging him since he had first talked to Marcel in 1978 – what had happened to the aliens?

Brigadier General Roger M. Ramey (left), Commander of Eighth Air Force, with the remains of the flying disk at his headquarters at Fort Worth, Texas.

In August 1989, while NBC were filming in Roswell, Friedman met retired mortician Glenn Dennis. He had worked for the Ballard Funeral Home, which had had a long-standing arrangement with Roswell Army Air Field, providing mortuary services. Glenn told Friedman about strange goings -on at the hospital on the base in the summer of 1947. The Army asked his advice on how to deal with 'small bodies'. The next time he turned up at the hospital he had been forcibly ejected, but a nurse at the base told him about 'very smelly' bodies she had seen being autopsied by two doctors. The corpses had brownish-grey skin and big heads with no hair. They had slits or holes for nose, ears and mouth and each hand had four slender fingers but no thumb. After several meetings with Dennis, the nurse suddenly disappeared. He had been told that she had moved to England but, when he tried to write to her, his letters were returned, stamped 'deceased'.

The episode of *Unsolved Mysteries* on the Roswell crash was aired in September 1989. It was seen across the US by twenty-eight million people. There followed a great wave of books and TV shows about Roswell.

In 1990 another witness who had seen the alien bodies came forward. An Army Air Forces photographer – who wished to be known only by the initials FB – approached Friedman, claiming to have seen the aliens' bodies recovered from the field in Corona. FB had been stationed at the Anacostia Naval Air Station, Washington, D.C, at the time. In July 1947, he and another photographer were ordered to fly to Roswell. When they arrived at RAAF, the two photographers were driven out to a tent in a field and told to photograph its contents.

'There were four bodies I could see,' FB says. 'They were not human; their heads appeared much too large for their tiny bodies.'

Friedman and others have come to believe that a second UFO had crashed around that time, on the plains of San Augustin, New Mexico, based on the testimony of two witnesses. One, Gerald Anderson, had contacted Friedman after seeing a 1990 re-run of the *Unsolved Mysteries* show. The other witness, Grady 'Barney' Barnett, had died by this time, but he had told the story to two friends, LaVerne and Jean Maltais, and they passed it on to Friedman independently.

The two stories matched. Both men said that alien bodies had been discovered in or around saucer debris. According to Anderson, one of the aliens survived the crash. Sadly, as Barnett was dead by then, he could not be questioned about this. As a result, a certain amount of doubt surrounds the San Augustin crash.

However, the details of the crash at Corona crash are now almost universally accepted. By the time Friedman's account

Remains of the flying disk, which allegedly crashed near Roswell, New Mexico.

Crash at Corona (co-written by aviation science writer Don Berliner) was published in 1992, most of the blanks in the story had been filled in.

In 1994, New Mexico Congressman Steven Schiff asked the US General Accounting Office to look into documents relating to the Corona–Roswell incident. When the Air Force heard about the GAO's investigation, they quickly issued their own twenty-five-page report admitting that they had lied about the weather-balloon story. In fact, what had crashed at Corona was a top-secret Mogul balloon designed to detect Soviet nuclear tests. However, the project was soon scrapped and declassified – so why did it take them so long to own up?

Lieutenant Haut has no time for this story either.

'Colonel Blanchard [the base commander who authorised Haut's press release] would have known about any secret experiments, or at least not to panic if anything odd fell from the sky,' he says. 'Why would he have authorised me to announce the story to the press? It just doesn't make sense.'

When the GAO's report was published in 1995, it reported that files relating to the crash had gone missing or been destroyed – to the point where the GAO could find no evidence of the crash at all. In response the USAF published *The Roswell Report: Truth Versus Fiction in the New Mexico Desert*. This was a simply an updated version of their first report, which makes no mention of the missing or destroyed files. However, it claims that the 'aliens' observed in the New Mexico desert were life-like test dummies, which had been dropped from a high-altitude balloon, and that the unusual military activity in the area at the time was simply the Air Force's attempt to recover them.

UFOlogists have universally discounted the USAF's explanation. However, some debunkers have come up with even weirder terrestrial explanations. It has been suggested that it was one of the nine thousand 'FUGO' balloons released by the Japanese in 1945. These were paper balloons that carried explosives. The idea was that they would drift over the Pacific and explode when they landed in America. But no one has been able to explain what it had been doing for the two years since the end of the war.

Some researchers have suggested that a rocket the US military were testing at the nearby White Sands Missile Range had gone astray. That might have fooled Mac Brazel, but surely the Army personnel at Roswell would have recognised a missile. The space programme – what there was of it at the time – was still under military control and some researchers claim that the 'alien bodies' were those of rhesus monkeys used in experiments to see how humans might cope with space travel.

In 1997, another reliable witness went public. A retired army officer, Philip J. Corso, had been a major in 1947. In early July, he had caught a corporal off-limit. The man was lurking in the shadows at the doorway of a warehouse on the base. His face was deathly white. The man was plainly frightened. He had disobeyed orders and was expecting to face severe discipline. He had been detailed to guard some crates that had been sent over from the army base at

Fort Bliss, Texas. They were marked top-secret. Breaking every rule in the book, he had opened some of the crates to take a look. What he had seen had scared him even more than the punishment he faced.

'You won't believe this,' he told Major Corso.

'What are you talking about?' asked Corso. There was no need for a reply. Inside the open crate, he saw the body of a strange creature.

'At first I thought it was a dead child they were shipping somewhere,' said Corso. 'It was a four-foot, human-shaped creature with bizarre-looking four-fingered hands… and a light-bulb shaped head. The eye sockets were oversized and almond-shaped and pointed down to its tiny nose, which didn't really protrude from its skull.'

Among the paperwork that accompanied the crate, Corso found an army intelligence report. It said that the creature had been recovered from a spacecraft that had crashed at Roswell, New Mexico, two days earlier. In the warehouse, there were over thirty other wooden crates that were part of the consignment. Major Corso slipped the lid back on and covered the crate with a tarpaulin. Outside he told the corporal: 'You never saw this and you tell no one.' Corso himself tried to forget what he had seen. But when the Roswell story broke, it brought it all back.

Corso is an unimpeachable witness. He spent twenty-one years in the army, serving alongside General Douglas MacArthur in Korea and later under President Eisenhower on the National Security Council, and was decorated nineteen times. After he left the service in 1963, he worked as an advisor on the staffs of US Senators Strom Thurmond and James Eastland and came to public attention when he testified to the House National Security Committee on the fate of US prisoners of war held in North Korea.

But not only has he testified to the fact that he saw a dead alien in 1947, he was to come across those mysterious packing cases again.

Crash in Arizona

Another UFO crash took place in Paradise Valley, Phoenix, Arizona, in 1947. A craft thirty-six feet in diameter was retrieved, along with two humanoid bodies.

Former businessman and pilot Selman E. Graves witnessed part of the recovery operation with two friends during a hunting trip.

'There were some mine shafts – what you might call an out-cropping – and a small hill, and we went up there and the three of us could look back and see everything that was taking place,' said Graves. 'There was a large – I can best describe it as a large aluminium dome-shaped thing there, which was roughly the size of a house – it was measured to be thirty-six feet in diameter.

'We could see that there were pitched buildings – tents – and men moving about. We at that time didn't have any idea what we were looking at. We thought it might be an observatory dome, except why would they have it down there on that piece of ground?'

Another informant named Silas Newton told Frank Scully, author of *Behind the Flying Saucers,* 'Supposedly there were a couple of small humanoids – about four-and-a-half feet tall – that were reported to be there.'

The Aztec Incident

Author Frank Scully also reported a crash that occurred near Aztec, New Mexico, in 1948. More dead aliens were retrieved. Most of Scully's information came from a 'Dr. Gee', who was in fact a composite of eight different people.

The disc that landed near Aztec was nearly a hundred feet in diameter and its exterior was made of a light metal resembling aluminium but was so durable that no amount of heat or diamond drilling had any effect. The craft was made from large rings of metal, which revolved around a central stabilised cabin, using an unfamiliar gear ratio. There were no rivets, bolts, screws or signs of welding. Investigators were eventually able to gain access to the craft by pushing a knob with a long pole through a porthole, which a hidden door to open. The craft was found to be assembled in segments using a complex system of grooves and pins. It was undamaged, having landed under its own guidance.

Sixteen small humanoids, ranging in height from thirty-six to forty-two inches, were found dead inside the cabin, their bodies charred to a dark brown colour. The craft and bodies were flown to Wright–Patterson Air Force Base.

In 1987, researcher William Steinman found some further evidence to support Scully's claim but refused to divulge his source. Steinman said that the crash had occurred on 25 March 1948 and was detected by three separate radar centres. It was the radar apparently that caused the craft to crash. In Steinman's version, only fourteen humanoid bodies were recovered and not sixteen as Scully had claimed.

Crash at Laredo

Another UFO crashed in Laredo, Texas, in the late 1940s. It was unearthed by Todd Zechel, of Ground Saucer Watch, who usually works with UFO documents he has obtained under the Freedom of Information Act. But in this case he got his information from an air force technician who was based at Carswell Air Force Base and chooses to remain anonymous.

The source says that on 7 July 1948, he had been involved in cordoning off an area near the town of Laredo. A ninety-foot disc had been downed in the area and was recovered. Radar operators and pilots witnessed the object as it flew over Albuquerque at an estimated speed of two thousand miles an hour.

Further evidence came from Leonard Stringfield, who learnt from other witnesses that a hairless four-foot entity had died in the crash and its body had been recovered. A US Navy officer also witnessed the wreckage being loaded onto trucks at the site.

Years later a photo was released of the dead 'alien'. However, this was quickly dismissed as a hoax. It showed a dead human pilot severely burned. Unfortunately the hoaxers did not realise that the photo also showed the dead man's sunglasses.

Government papers since released indicate that the Air Force were experimenting with modified Nazi V2 rockets at the time. The 'alien', it is said, was a monkey.

Alien Autopsy

While the USAF continues to deny that a UFO crashed at Roswell, there is evidence that yet another UFO may have been downed in New Mexico that year. Since 1995, television stations in over thirty countries have broadcast portions of what is said to be an alien autopsy. The alien in the film appears to match the eyewitness descriptions and sketches made by Roswell mortician Glenn Dennis from what his contact, the Air Force nurse, had told him. London-based film producer Ray Santilli, who claims to have bought the film from the cameraman, says that several military personnel involved in 1947 have confirmed that the alien is the creature recovered from a saucer crash in New Mexico. However, the cameraman claimed to have taken the footage on 31 May 1947, near Socorro, New Mexico, three days before the crash at Roswell.

Display on alien autopsy in a UFO museum at Roswell, New Mexico, USA.

The film was first aired in America on 28 August 1995, when ten million television viewers watched the documentary, *Alien Autopsy: Fact or Fiction*, on the Fox Network. It comprised a series of grainy, black-and-white film segments, which were said to be archive footage from 1947. In the footage, pathologists are shown carefully dissecting what appears to be an alien life form.

The film begins with a military officer showing pieces of debris to the camera. Unfortunately, neither his face nor any insignia that would identify his rank or unit are shown. Next the staircase and doorway to the autopsy room are shown. The camera then sweeps around the naked body of an alien lying on a table. It is bald and hairless, with a rounded stomach and no evidence of genitals. The pathologist then enters, wearing a biohazard suit, and begins his grisly work.

Deep incisions were made in the neck and chest. The skin was then drawn back and the creature's internal organs removed. Then the skin was removed from the top of the head. The skull was sawn open and the brain removed. During the autopsy, a figure can be seen behind an observation window. Santilli maintains that this is President Truman.

Santilli says he discovered the autopsy footage when he had been researching a music documentary. In the summer of 1993, he came across some previously unseen Elvis Presley footage in Cleveland, Ohio. After arranging the cash to buy the Presley film, the cameraman offered Santilli some other footage that he shot during his time in the forces. Santilli was told that the film was 'valuable' and a screening was arranged. He was impressed. The film showed a UFO crash site, and the autopsy of the extraterrestrials who had died in the crash. By November 1994, Santilli had raised another $150,000 to buy the film.

Back in Britain, Santilli took the film to the British UFO Research Association and showed it to Philip Mantle, BUFORA's director of research. Mantle was convinced by what he saw.

'The footage is unique,' he said. 'It is the only known instance of aliens on film.' On 26 March 1995, BUFORA issued a press release. In it, Mantle said: 'We have had the film checked out by

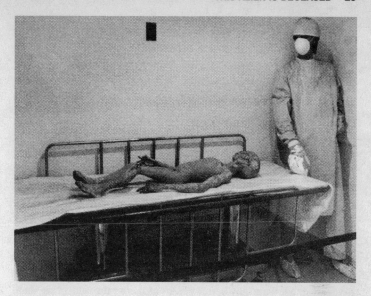

Display showing an alien autopsy (with models) at a UFO museum in Roswell, New Mexico, USA.

Kodak who confirm it is fifty years old... we now plan to have it examined by film experts at Sheffield.'

However, some people in the UFO community smelt a rat. The editor of *UFO Magazine* Graham Birdsall phoned Peter Milson, a senior manager with Kodak in England. Milson knew nothing of BUFORA's press release claiming that Kodak had verified the date of the film. Birdsall began ringing round other Kodak offices. None of them admitted carrying out any tests on the alien autopsy film. After four months, Birdsall found a salesman at Kodak's Copenhagen office, who had been approached by someone on Santilli's behalf. He asked whether the film-edge markings, a square and triangle, meant the year of manufacture was 1947. The salesman checked back through Kodak's film logs and confirmed that this was correct. However, the salesman did not realise that the same edge markings also appeared on film manufactured in 1927 and 1967. Kodak's Peter Milson then went to great pains to point out to Santilli that 'the date of manufacture does not confirm the date when the film was shot or processed'.

Kodak could confirm the date of the film and offered to do so. What they would need were two frames of the autopsy sequence. But when the alien autopsy footage appeared on TV in August 1995, Kodak said that no frames had been forthcoming.

Santilli insists that Kodak had tested the film and confirmed the age of the footage. However, Kodak's motion-picture specialist Tony Amato, who would have directed the authentication process, says that, despite promises from Santilli through a US intermediary, Kodak has never received a single frame of the alien autopsy film.

Other UFOlogists expressed their concern that the film was doing their case more harm than good. They were particularly concerned that UFO researchers with established credentials in the Roswell crash were not being given access to the film. Nor were they being given the facts behind the story.

Undeterred, German UFO researcher Michael Hesemann began his own investigation and published his findings in *Facts v Polemics in the Alien Autopsy Footage Debate*. According to Hesemann, two three-frame segments were submitted for tests to the editor of the photography magazine *Shutterbug*, Bob Shell, who had been a photographic consultant for the US legal system and for the FBI.

Shell made a careful chemical analysis of the film's make-up and confirmed that it had been manufactured before 1956. The film was Super XX-Panchromatic 16mm Safety Film, an indoor, high-speed film, which was unstable. It had a life span of no more than two years. So the film had to be shot and developed before 1958. That meant the film could well be genuine. The problem was that the segments Shell tested did not show the alien, so some doubts still hung over the film's authenticity.

Meanwhile, attention turned to the cameraman who had taken the film. He did not want his identity revealed, but under the pseudonym 'Jack Barnett' he issued a statement explaining how he had come to shoot the film. In the summer of 1947, 'Barnett' was stationed in Washington, D.C., when he received orders to make his way to New Mexico to film the crash site of a Russian spy plane. On the way, he stopped off at Wright Field in Ohio to pick up the equipment he would need. From Wright Field he flew to Roswell, then travelled by road through the desert to the crash site. In his 1995 statement, Barnett was vague about the location of the crash site, but later he led Michael Hesemann to a site near Socorro, New Mexico. And he said that the crash had occurred on 31 May 1947, not in July 1947 when the UFO had crashed at Corona.

Kent Jeffrey, head of the International Roswell Initiative, a UFO research group, was also on the case. He noted that Barnett's statement was full of British expressions, not the sort of language that an American would have used. He tracked down a number of retired combat cameramen who had been in the service in 1947. They included retired Air Force Lieutenant Colonel Daniel A. McGovern, a motion-picture project officer for the Air Force, who filmed the devastation of Nagasaki after the atomic bomb was dropped on it in 1945 and was stationed in Washington, D.C, in June 1947 when the cameraman of the alien autopsy was there, and Bill Gibson, who filmed the B-25 bombers taking off from the air-craft carrier *Hornet* to make the famous 'Doolittle raid' on Japan in April 1942. All of them had worked on top secret projects. They said it made no sense to fly a cameraman from Washington to New Mexico to film the crash site. There were qualified cameramen with high-level security clearances stationed across the country. If a UFO had crashed in New Mexico, combat cameramen would have been despatched from Roswell Army Air Field itself.

McGovern had filmed a number of conventional autopsies during his career. He maintained that all medical procedures were routinely shot in colour. The alien autopsy was shot in grainy monochrome. The hand-held film is shaky and out of focus. The veterans say that the quality of the camera work is appalling, well below the standard required in the military.

'If anybody in my unit shot film in that manner, he'd be back scrubbing pots in the kitchen,' said Joe Longo, President of the International Combat Camera Association.

Colonel McGovern offered to check out the cameraman. He was prepared to do this in conditions of the strictest confidentiality. However, he would need the cameraman's full name and serial number to access his military service file in the Air Force Records Center. However, Santilli, respecting the cameraman's right to privacy, said: 'I can state quite categorically that the last person the cameraman is going to place any confidence in is an ex-military serviceman… in the present climate the cameraman will be doing himself and his family a disservice by going public… However good his credentials, he will be torn limb from limb.'

Critics claim that Santilli is deliberately obstructing their efforts to find out the truth. But given the media feeding frenzy that accompanies any fresh development in the Roswell case, it seems quite reasonable that the cameraman should want to protect his privacy. Those who take the footage at face value point to attacks on its authenticity as another example of the authorities covering up the facts about UFOs by discrediting genuine evidence and credible witnesses with a campaign of smear and disinformation that ultimately turns public attention from the issue.

However, whether the alien autopsy film is genuine or a hoax, it did do one valuable thing. It revived interest in the whole issue of UFOs. What's more, there are plenty of UFOlogists who stick up for the film.

'We've got surgeons saying that the creature in the film was flesh and blood,' says Philip Mantle of BUFORA. 'We've got military personnel who recognise the alien as the same thing they saw in 1947. It fits.'

Survivor?
While researchers were arguing about the authenticity of the alien autopsy film, evidence emerged that not all the alien astronauts had perished in the 1947 UFO crashes. At least one, it seemed, survived long enough to be interviewed. Another remarkable piece of footage showing an alien being interrogated surfaced. Just under three minutes long, it was said to have been smuggled out of the Nellis Air Force Range and Nuclear Test Site – the home of the

secret establishment known as Area 51. The footage clearly shows two men cross-questioning an ailing extraterrestrial.

Area 51 first came to the attention of the public in 1989, when Robert 'Bob' Lazar, a physicist who had worked there, claimed that the US military were building nine flying saucers there, based on downed craft in their possession. His revelation produced a vicious backlash from the authorities, though they subsequently admitted that Area 51 exists.

The alien interrogation footage was stolen from the Groom Lake complex by a man known as 'Victor', who also worked there. He said that the film was a clipping from hundreds of hours of interview footage showing the many different species of extraterrestral held at Area 51.

A few seconds of the tape were aired in April 1997 on the US TV show *Strange Universe*. This provoked a massive media reaction and reawakened public interest in Area 51. But the question in everyone's mind was, was it true?

The film was first shown to TV network executive Robert Kiviat, who made the documentary *Alien Autopsy: Fact or Fiction*. He turned it down on the grounds that he had already had his fingers burnt in the row over the authenticity of the alien autopsy film. Other producers were equally wary. However, Rocket Pictures Home Video of Los Angeles were making a documentary investigating claims that the US government were employing extraterrestrials on top-secret technology projects at Area 51. Rocket's president, Tom Coleman, stepped in and bought the footage. Independent producer and UFO enthusiast Jeff Broadstreet was called in to make a show around the three-minute clip. He lined up a group of experts to view the film. Among them were distinguished UFO researchers and writers Whitley Strieber, Sean Morton and Major Robert Dean, along with two leading Hollywood special-effects men.

The alien interview footage had been shot through a pane of glass and there was no sound. It showed an interview taking place in a darkened room that was lit with an eerie greenish glow. It is possible to make out the silhouettes of two men, sitting with their backs to the camera at one end of a long table, which was covered with microphones and wires. One was wearing a military uniform. There appear to be stars on the epaulets of his jacket. The other man was more casually dressed and occasionally rubbed his forehead with his hand.

At the other end of the table sat a small, beige-skinned creature with black eyes and a bulbous head – 'the likes of which haunt the nightmares of thousands of unwilling abductees,' said Sean Morton, who was amazed by the footage.

The creature appeared to be unwell. It seemed to be hooked up to medical monitors. One was blinking erratically, as if it were monitoring a very sickly heart. Its bulbous head looked purple and bruised, and it bobbed and jerked involuntarily. Towards the end of the footage, the creature suffers some form of seizure. Its mouth snapped open and closed rapidly as some kind of fluid dribbled from it. The heart monitor went wild, and two medics rushed in. One of them cradled the alien's head and pointed a pen-light into its eyes. The other put his fingers into its mouth, apparently in an attempt to help it breathe. At this point, the footage comes to an abrupt end.

In August 1997, Rocket released their documentary *Area 51: The Alien Interview*. It showed the footage and a discussion between the expert witnesses.

'Rocket tried to make a balanced documentary,' said producer Jeff Broadstreet, 'and so have contrasted the comments of Morton and Dean, who both believe the footage to be genuine, against two of Hollywood's leading special-effects experts, who both thought the video was a hoax and that the ET was either digitally created or a mechanical puppet.'

This left Broadstreet sitting on the fence. 'Personally, I don't know if it's real or not,' he says. And he does not believe the matter is ever going to be settled one way or the other. 'I mean, who's going to be able to authenticate whether the footage of a live ET is real? Even if the government had footage of a live ET, do you think they are going to admit it?'

The documentary sparked a debate about the authenticity of the footage. Like the cameraman of the alien autopsy, Victor is publicity shy. In the documentary he appeared only in silhouette.

'He won't tell us his real name,' says Broadstreet. 'He won't tell us in what official capacity he worked at Area 51, only that he was definitely there. He told me that his biggest fear is if the authorities discover his identity and he wants, at all costs, to avoid the trouble Bob Lazar attracted.'

Although the original video had a soundtrack, Victor removed the soundtrack from the tape before going public to hide the identity of the two men interrogating the creature. Victor said that the man in the military uniform was 'some kind of aide', while the civilian was a government telepath.

Victor thought that the alien died later from its injuries, though he was not sure. He did know that it was not interviewed again. Victor also said it was not the only alien at Area 51. He had seen them on other occasions but he does not know, or cannot say, whether they had been captured from crashed UFOs or were working at the base voluntarily.

Unfortunately, the original videotape was not available for examination as Victor had smuggled the footage out of Area 51 on a computer disk, after converting it into digital format. Nevertheless, computer image analyst Jim Dilettoso examined the footage frame by frame. He believes that it was not shot on video, as Victor had claimed, but on film stocks, as no interference patterns were shown on the monitor in the shot. But he admits that this could also be explained if the interview was videoed 'under very low lighting conditions'.

The two Hollywood special effects technicians called in thought the footage was a hoax and said that they could have done much better. Four-time Oscar winner Rick Baker said: 'It's definitely a puppet and not a very well done one either. It's very much like a guy's got his hand inside the thing, manoeuvring it… It looks like they took a great deal of effort to hide as much of the anatomy as possible. I'd be willing to stake my reputation on this being a hoax. It's a fake.'

However, John Criswell does have some doubts.

'Just when I was sure it was some kind of puppet, it would start to lift up, jerk or move in such a way that would be very difficult to fake,' he says.

Whitley Strieber, author of *Communion and Transformations*, who claims to be a multiple abductee, also believes the tape is a fake, but was distressed by the way the creature – fake or not – was being treated. It invokes memories of his own abductions.

'It is very difficult to watch this,' he said, 'because somebody who made this knows something about the way they move.' He never wants to see the footage again.

Morton was 'utterly amazed' by the footage and was very concerned by the condition of the alien. He was particularly interested in the time code that appears on the video. It is prefaced by the letters DNI. Morton believes that Area 51 is run by the Department of Naval Intelligence. This had been the conclusion of George Knapp, who had spent a year investigating the claims of Bob Lazar. Lazar's pay cheques had had the letters DNI printed on them and his tax statement for 1989 showed that he was employed by the Department of Naval Intelligence.

But the video's most enthusiastic supporter was Colonel Bob Dean, generally regarded as one of the most important UFO researchers from the military.

'I was quite prepared to see a hoax,' he said, 'yet what I saw took me completely by surprise. It had a profound emotional impact on me. I became convinced that this was the real thing.' He, too, reacted angrily to the way the alien was being treated.

Dean says the alien in the interview video 'matches with other photographs of ETs I have seen'. Dean also believes that the alien autopsy film is genuine because the creature depicted looks exactly like pictures he had seen of alien bodies recovered from UFO crashes he had privileged access to in the military.

'I happen to know the autopsy film is real,' he says, 'because the footage sold to producer Ray Santilli was released over twenty years ago to our military allies in the South East Asia Organisation. He also believes that the release of the autopsy film was no accident. It was part of a CIA plan to gauge and manipulate public opinion.

'I know that the level of classification on this kind of material is so far beyond top secret that you can't imagine how tightly the government sits on it,' he says.

Nevertheless, he can quite understand why other UFOlogists are sceptical about the alien interview video, and he compares it to the reaction of people when they first saw the extraterrestrial in the autopsy film.

'Just because it didn't look like a "typical Grey", or whatever it's expected to look like, they immediately thought it was fake,' says Dean. 'The alien creature in the interview video is not one of the typical-looking Greys either, but people don't realise we are not dealing with one but several different species.'

The sceptics are lead by UFO researcher Michael Lindemann.

'There is no compelling reason to consider it real,' he says. 'Therefore it has to be a fake. I know of a number of people who have seen the entire tape, who have said that it's a hoax.'

Lindemann saw the 'same stupid three seconds on *Strange Universe* as everyone else' and was so angry at the show's lack of balance that he called the producers and complained.

'I think the whole character of Victor is highly dubious,' Lindemann said. 'There's not even a hint of authenticity when he was interviewed. I believe Rocket Home Video are looking for a quick killing.'

This serves to highlight the problem that controversial evidence, such as the alien autopsy and the alien interview, poses for UFOlogists. If they are shown to be fake, it dents the credibility of the whole phenomenon. And where alien footage is concerned, the allegation can always be made that they have been cleverly faked in the hope of making money.

The Kingman Crash

The New Mexico, Arizona and Texas crashes of 1947 and 1948 were not the only times that UFOs have come to Earth. According to US scientist Fritz Werner, a UFO crashed just south of the Grand Canyon national park at Kingman, Arizona, in 1953. Werner had first-hand knowledge of the crash because he was one of the scientists sent to investigate the wreckage. At the time, Werner was part of a top-secret team of scientists working in the deserts of Nevada. Their assignment was to make a scientific assessment of blast damage caused by a nuclear test.

On 20 May 1953, Werner was called aside by the physicist incharge of the research group. He was to catch a special flight to Phoenix, Arizona. At the airfield, he was picked up by a large bus with blacked-out windows. There were fifteen other passengers on board, and they were ordered to remain silent during their journey out into the desert.

The bus arrived at their destination on the evening of 21 May. When the passengers alighted they were escorted to a canyon where huge arc lights illuminated a large disc that was guarded by a detachment of soldiers. The disc was around thirty feet in diameter. It was embedded into the sandy soil and stuck out of the ground at an angle.

Werner was told to calculate the impact speed of the object. He did this and reported his findings, and then he was told to go back to the bus to await transportation back to Nevada. On the way, he managed to sneak a quick peek inside a tent. Inside, to his amazement, he saw the body of an alien. It had brownish skin and was about four feet tall, and it was dressed in a silver one-piece suit complete with skull-cap.

Werner was told that the disc he had seen was a highly classified US jet fighter that had crashed in the desert. He did not believe this. As the years passed, nothing remotely like it went into service, and in 1973, although Werner had signed a declaration of secrecy, he contacted eminent UFOlogist Ray Fowler. Unfortunately, as no-one outside the military knew anything about the crash at Roswell at the time, Fowler could shed no light on what Werner had seen. However, four years later, Fowler's colleague Leonard Stringfield heard an account from another witness that seemed to corroborate Werner's story.

The second witness was a former National Guard pilot who wished to remain anonymous. In the 1950s, he had been stationed at the Wright–Patterson Air Force Base in Dayton, Ohio. Between

1948 and 1969, Wright Field was the home of the US government UFO research project. It also housed the Foreign Technology Division. The job of FTD specialists was to unravel the mysteries of enemy technology that had fallen into US hands. Usually this meant examining the wreckage of the latest crashed Soviet MiG jet and working out enemy capabilities, but there were rumours that the technicians there also worked on technology collected from more exotic sources. A secret US Air Force intelligence document outlined Project Moon Dust, which was responsible for collecting any Soviet space debris that fell to Earth. It also mentions that, as part of these 'FTD Projects… qualified field intelligence person-nel' were to be posted on 'a quick reaction basis to recover or per-form field exploration of Unidentified Flying Objects'.

One day in mid-1953, some crates were delivered to Wright–Patterson containing items retrieved from the Arizona desert, the airman said. Inside there was wreckage from a crash. The airman said that some of it had strange writing on it in sym-bols that resembled Sanskrit. Other crates contained the bodies of three aliens, packed into dry-ice containers to preserve the tissues. They were about four feet tall, with large heads and parchment-like skin – almost identical to the one Werner had seen. And they had come from Arizona.

A data file hacked from the mainframe at Wright–Patterson con-tains a description of the aliens by Dr Frederick Hauser. He said that the creatures were 'eerily human-like' though 'smaller than average in size, and completely bald. No eyebrows or eyelashes. No body hair at all.'

Another scientist who has examined alien remains recovered from a downed UFO is Dr Robert Sarbacher. In 1986, he said that their bodies were extremely light 'constructed like certain insects we have observed on Earth, wherein, because of the low mass, the inertial forces involved would be quite low'. This would explain how the creatures survived high-G aerial manoeuvres. It also matches the descriptions given by many eyewitnesses who have come face-to-face with aliens.

Crash at Kecksburg

Another UFO crashed in 1965 near Kecksburg, Pennsylvania. At 4:45 p.m. on the afternoon of 9 December 1965, a fiery object was seen flying across the skies above the Great Lakes on the US–Canadian border. Numerous witnesses saw it and reported what they had seen to the authorities. They said they had seen an orange mass with smoke trailing from it and pieces falling off it. Some mistook what they saw for an aircraft that was on fire, though their accounts more accurately resembled meteorite breaking up high above the earth – an explanation often given for UFO sightings.

However, later the same evening, a loud sonic boom was heard in the area of Kecksburg and a powerful tremor shook the ground as something crash-landed in a nearby wood. It left behind it a thick trail of smoke that remained in the sky for twenty minutes. This could be seen from Pontiac, Michigan, some two hundred miles away, where it was filmed.

It was certainly not a meteorite. Scientist Ivan Sanderson collected the sighting reports and found some extraordinary anomalies. According to eyewitnesses, the UFO took six minutes to cover a few hundred miles. Meteorites travel much faster than that. By plotting the sightings on a map, it was possible to show that the object veered to the east before it crashed. Meteorites cannot change direction. If the object that crashed into the wood was not a meteorite, perhaps it was a piece of space junk. Sanderson discovered that a Soviet rocket, Cosmos 96, had indeed re-entered that day. But NORAD, the early warning system in Colorado, reported the re-entry thirteen hours before the crash at Kecksburg.

The local emergency services rushed to the crash site, expecting to find the wreckage of plane. Instead, the firemen saw a strange, cone-shaped object. But the military soon arrived and took over, so they assumed that the object was part of a crashed military jet.

The military claimed that they had found nothing in the forest that night and dismissed the UFO sighting reports that had been made in the area. However, in 1980, Kecksburg fire chief Robert Bitner told local UFO investigators Clark McClelland and Stan Gordon what he had seen. On the evening of 9 December 1965,

Bitner and assistant fire chief James Mayes had entered the woods, expecting to find a scene of devastation left by a plane crash. Instead, they found a conical craft – about ten or twelve feet high – embedded in the ground.

The flying saucer had crashed into the woods at an angle of about 30 degrees. It had knocked the tops off trees and flattened the undergrowth. Despite the evidence of the severity of the crash, it had not caught fire and was virtually intact. There was a circle on the base of the craft. On it there were what looked like symbols or some form of writing. Bitner and his team had had plenty of time to examine the craft, before the military arrived and escorted them out of the woods. They knew what they saw.

Assistant fire chief Mayes also talked to McClelland and Stan Gordon and confirmed what Bitner had said. According to Mayes, a flat-bed truck had left the site later that night. It was carrying a large object covered with a tarpaulin. Mayes has no doubt that the US military removed the strange object they had seen, then denied that they had found anything in the woods as part of a cover-up.

Later, an officer at Lockbourne Air Force Base near Columbus, Ohio, which is about 150 miles from Kecksburg, told researchers that a flat-bed truck carrying a large conical object, covered by a tarpaulin, arrived at Lockbourne before dawn on 10 December 1965. The truck entered by a little-used back gate where the officer had been posted. He was ordered to shoot anyone who tried to get near the truck. At 7 a.m., the truck and its mysterious load left for Wright–Patterson Air Force Base – home of UFO research project and the FTD unit. The officer was never told what was under the tarpaulin. But are there reasons to believe that it was an extraterrestrial craft?

Mysterious Cargo

Another mysterious cargo had turned up at Fort Riley, Kansas, exactly a year earlier. On 10 December 1964, a guard on duty in the motor pool and three other men were ordered by a senior officer to make their way to a remote corner of the base.

When they arrived, they noticed a large military chopper shining a large searchlight on a strange object which was resting on the ground. The object was already surrounded by other military personnel. The guard was given orders to stop any civilians who tried to get near it. He was told to 'shot to kill' if necessary. He was also warned not to tell anyone about the incident.

The object looked something like a giant hamburger, forty foot by sixteen foot, with a dark line along its rim and a small tail-fin stabiliser. The guard noticed that the air near the craft was very warm despite it being a bitterly cold night.

Some time later, UFO researchers managed to obtain some corroboration of his story. Another guard reported that on the next morning, he saw a large flat-bed truck with a roundish object covered with canvas sheets being driven out of the base under high security.

The Port Ness Monster

UFOs do not only crash in America. At 4:10 p.m. on 26 October 1996, a bright light, trailing smoke and fire, was seen moving across the sky from the Port of Ness at the northern tip of the Isle of Lewis in the Outer Hebrides. Suddenly it exploded over the sea. Eyewitnesses saw two large pieces of debris spiral down towards the water, leaving a trail of smoke. As they hit the water, they exploded again, so violently that the surface of the sea was ablaze for several minutes.

The coastguards at nearby Stornoway were alerted, and lifeboats were quickly dispatched to the scene. Transatlantic airline routes pass over Lewis, and the authorities feared that a plane had crashed. It was quickly established that no planes, military or civilian, were missing. Nevertheless, an RAF Nimrod was sent to join the surface craft searching the dark waters. The search was wound up the next day, without result. 'It has been a fairly massive search, but a complete blank has been drawn,' said an RAF spokesman. 'We remain puzzled by what could have caused this.'

However, it was only the public search that was over. Civilian vessels were quickly moved out of the waters around Lewis. The official reason for this was that a naval exercise was taking place in the area. The fact that it began the day after a UFO had been downed was purely coincidental, of course. A fleet of military aircraft, ships and submarines converged on the area. Later, fishermen saw a naval frigate hauling wreckage up from the ocean floor. Apparently something had been found.

Four months later, in April 1997, an unidentified substance, possibly a fuel residue, washed up on Tangusdale Beach on Barra, at the southern end of the Outer Hebrides. Local seamen confirmed that, given the currents and prevailing winds, this substance could well have taken that long to have been carried down from the northern tip of Lewis.

Downed in Nebraska

It is not even as if UFO crashes were new. On 6 June 1884, a blazing object fell from the skies above Dundy County in southern Nebraska. Seeing the object hit the ground, local farmhands ran to the scene. They found a large area of scorched vegetation and that the ground had been fused into glass. In the middle of devastation was a mass of smouldering metal. One man got too close. His skin blistered in a way reminiscent of radiation burns. It took several days before the wreckage was cool enough to touch. The debris, it was found, was as strong as brass, but incredibly light. It seemed to have the characteristics of aluminium alloys, unknown in the 1880s. The local press at the time speculated that the strange craft had come from outer space.

The Bodies from Brazil

The alien seen in the alien interview video may not have been the only extraterrestrial to survive a crash. In 1996, two aliens were captured in Brazil. Despite medical care they do not seem to have survived and their remains, like those of other extraterrestrials, seem to have ended up in the hands of the American government.

The story began at 8 a.m. on the morning of Saturday 20 January 1996, when the fire department of Varginha – a city of 180,000 inhabitants in the Minais Gerais state of Brazil – received an anonymous telephone call. The caller had seen a mysterious creature in a park in the northern suburb of Jardim Andere. In Varginha, it was not unusual for dangerous wild animals to wander into populated areas, and the fire department was responsible for dealing with such incidents. They were in no great hurry. Two hours later, a fire truck eventually arrived at Jardim Andere and parked on the brow of a hill overlooking the park. A number of journalists were already on the scene, interviewing eyewitnesses.

The five fire officers were expecting to deal with a wild animal so, equipped with nets and cages, they made their way down the slope into the park. In the woodlands there, they found a small biped crouching in the trees. It was three foot tall with strange oily-brown skin. The strange creature had three raised humps on its forehead, blood-red eyes and a small opening for a mouth. It also gave off a strange buzzing sound, like a swarm of bees, and it appeared to be injured.

The fire-fighters were ill equipped to deal with an injured alien. The officer called the local army base. The commandant, General Sergio Coelho Lima, despatched troops who sealed off the area, but builder's assistant Henrique Jose saw what happened next from the rooftop of a nearby house. Four firemen trapped the creature in their nets. Then they transferred it to a wooden crate, which they handed over to the military. Everyone seemed pleased with the efficiency of the operation.

What no one had realised was that there was not just one alien on the loose in Varginha, but two. Later that day, local UFO investigator Ubirijara Franco Rodrigues – who was unaware of the first incident – began getting calls reporting another bizarre sighting. These led him to interview three girls who had stumbled across a strange creature crouching outside a building on Benevenuto Bras Vieira Street in the Jardim Andere district, near to where the first creature had been captured. They had seen the creature at around 3:30 p.m. on their way back from work as housemaids.

The girls – Liliane Fatima Silva, sixteen, her sister Valquira, fourteen, and a friend Katia Andrade Xavier, twenty-two – told Rodrigues that the creature they had seen looked like the devil, with three raised humps on its forehead. They ran screaming from the scene.

'It was not animal or human,' Katia said. 'It was a horrible thing.'

Harvard psychologist Dr John Mack interviewed the three girls later and is convinced they are telling the truth. 'If I am wrong,' he said. 'I will tear up my diploma.'

The three girls ran as fast as they could to the house of Luisa Silva, the mother of two of the girls. The news spread like wildfire. Soon terrified residents were calling the fire department reporting a second creature on the loose.

'The witnesses are very reliable,' said Rodrigues. 'There are signs of emotional trauma caused by the strange meeting with the alien.'

The second creature also appeared to be injured. The authorities moved quicker this time. Again fire officers netted the unfortunate creatures, and the army whisked it away. But this capture took place on the street and they could not prevent a crowd gathering to watch.

Soon Ubirijara Franco Rodrigues hooked up with a fellow UFO researcher Rodrigues e Pacaccini, who was investigating the morning sightings, but knew nothing of the second incident. At first there was some confusion, but two UFOlogists eventually realised that they were investigating two separate – though connected – alien sightings and decided to pool their resources. The first thing they needed was more witnesses, so they began distributing flyers.

Although Varginha is three hundred miles from Rio de Janeiro, rumours that the authorities had captured two aliens soon reached the Brazilian UFO publications there. Every UFO researcher in Brazil beat a path to Varginha to investigate. The local press also appealed for witnesses. Public meetings were held. Soon over sixty eyewitnesses had come forward – and a substantial proportion were in the military. From the beginning it was plain that two extra-terrestrials had indeed been captured. But what the investigators wanted to know was what had happened to them. As the eyewitness accounts were pieced together, a clear picture began to emerge.

ness accounts were pieced together, a clear picture began to emerge.

It appears that the first creature was taken to the School of the Sergeant at Arms – a military school – at Tres Coracoes, south east of Varginha. The authorities then refused to say what happened to it afterwards. However, investigators discovered that a policeman who had been involved in its capture on Saturday night had been injured. Two days later, he died in hospital. The cause of death was given as pneumonia but, when the dead man's family pushed for more details, the hospital authorities refused to discuss the matter further.

Rodrigues and Pacaccini established that the second creature had been taken to Varginha Regional Hospital, late on Saturday afternoon. Either that day or the following morning, the creature was transferred to Varginha's Humanitas Hospital two miles away. The doctors there were apparently better equipped to deal with its injuries. Nevertheless, the creature died in Humanitas Hospital at 6 p.m. on Monday, 22 January. According to a military source, the alien's autopsy was performed there. At least fifteen doctors, military, police and fire officers crowded into the room to see the creature laid out in a wooden casket. Apparently, one of the doctors prised open the alien's tiny mouth, pushed a pair of forceps inside and pulled out its tongue, which was black. When he let go, the tongue sprang back.

Those who saw the corpse said the creature had three fingers and three raised humps on its forehead. It had no navel, no nipples and no sexual organs. Its skin was brown and oily in texture, matching other eyewitness descriptions. And its legs, which appeared to be jointed, were grazed and wrinkled.

When the lid to the casket was screwed down, two military figures wearing face masks and gloves wrapped the coffin in black plastic sheeting, then placed it on the back of a truck. Early the following morning, a convoy of army trucks headed out of Varginha. The indications are that alien's body was taken to the University of Campinas, Unicamp, two hundred miles south-west of Varginha. Nothing more is known about what happened to the creature.

Pacaccini interviewed a Brazilian Air Force radar operator, who

Forces had been alerted by the US. They were tracking a UFO that was entering Brazilian airspace. The Americans gave details of the craft's trajectory, but they could not say whether the UFO was intending to land or was about to crash.

In the days leading up to 20 January, Varginha had been a hotbed of UFO sightings. Hundreds had been reported in the area. Aliens had also been seen. Farmer Eurico de Freitas and his wife had been woken in the early hours of the morning by the sound of disturbed farm animals. Looking out from their bedroom window, they saw a grey object, emitting 'some kind of smoke', move silently across the fields about sixteen feet above the ground, before disappearing into the night.

Pacaccini did not discount the possibility that the two creatures in captivity might have been human in origin – maybe the result of a military experiment that had gone badly wrong. But if the creatures captured in Varginha were genuine extraterrestrials, where was their spacecraft? Pacaccini's efforts to trace the wreckage have been stonewalled by the military, and he claims there has been an official cover up. He has also received countless death threats by anonymous callers. If anyone in the military so much as mentions his name, they risk an immediate ten-day detention. General Lima ordered a security clamp-down as leaks from the military provoked what the local papers called 'ET mania'. He issued an order banning anyone under his command from speaking to any Brazilian UFOlogist. But this has not prevented further details about the case being leaked to researchers.

It has since come to the investigators' attention that an American was present on the morning of 20 January when the first creature was captured and loaded on to the military truck. And a C-5 or C-17 US Air Force transport plane was seen later that day at Sao Paulo International Airport. Two days later, an American transport – probably the same plane – appeared at Campinas Airport, which is close to the University where the second creature was taken after its autopsy. The indications are that the creatures – one possibly still alive, the other dead – were flown to the US in the care of the American military.

American military.

In that case they may have missed a third creature on the loose. In February 1996, a local van driver was driving round a curve when his headlights picked out a strange creature some fifty-five yards away. The driver screeched to a halt. He saw the creature raise its arms to cover its 'blood-red eyes' and run off into the night. The driver said that it had either four or three fingers on each hand.

Two months later, on the evening of 21 April, sixty-seven-year-old Mrs Terezinha Gallo Clepf was dining at the restaurant in Varingha Zoo when, at 9 p.m., she went outside for a cigarette. She came face-to-face with a creature matching the description of the others seen in the area. This immediately spawned speculation that more extraterrestrials had arrived in Varginha and were looking for their friends.

Also in April 1996, Luisa Silva, mother of two of the girls who first witnessed the second creature, got a visit from the 'Men in Black' – though, this being Latin America, they were men in white. Four strangers – none of whom were Brazilian – wearing white or cream Armani suits turned up at her home. They offered her 'a large sum of cash' to persuade her daughters to deny what they had seen. Mrs Silva refused and the men drove off in a blue 1994 Lincoln Continental car. They promised to return.

Since the incident in Varginha, Brazil's leading UFO magazine has discovered that the office phones have been bugged.

'We have received confirmation of this from a reliable source,' says editor A.J. Gevaerd. 'We have always condemned the world-wide cover-up surrounding UFOs, and the Roswell case. But there isn't a single article in the Brazilian Constitution that prohibits UFOlogical research – and that's enough reason for us to continue.'

Despite the dangers, Gevaerd continues investigating the aliens of Varginha.

'It has been a breakthrough in Brazilian UFOlogy,' he says. 'To our happiness, it happened right in Varginha. I think it will be the first step towards a global change of consciousness regarding the subject of UFOs.'

Russia's Roswell

In the closing months of 1998, some footage emerged that proved that extraterrestials were visiting Earth. Not only that, it showed that a crashed alien spacecraft and some dead aliens were in the possession of a superpower. But this time the extraterrestrials had not fallen into the hands of the US. The Soviets had got them.

A series of segments of colour film have been found in the files of the KGB and were aired on the US cable channel TNT on 13 September 1998. The footage shows a disc-shaped alien spacecraft that had crashed into the Sverdlovsk region of Western Siberia some time in March 1969. In one segment, Russian military personnel and KGB officers are shown inspecting the crash site. In the foreground, a large fragment of disc juts from the frozen Soviet soil. Another segment shows the autopsy of a badly mutilated creature recovered from the wreck. Three men in surgical garb are shown setting to work on its headless torso and arm.

In the KGB films the surgical work on the unfortunate extraterrestrial was frighteningly realistic. This time it was in focus and, unlike the American alien autopsy movie, the faces of the people in the footage can be clearly made out. However, although these men can be identified, tracking down former military personnel in the former Soviet Union is no easy task. Although the film has passed all sorts of tests, UFO researchers are reluctant to attest to its authenticity, just in case.

Alien Grave

One of the strangest cases involving a crashed UFO occurred more than a hundred years ago in the town of Aurora, Texas. The year was 1897, during which the US was plagued with hundreds of sightings of strange airships.

The story goes that on 19 April 1897 a strange airship appeared over the town of Aurora. The craft then apparently crashed into a windmill tower and exploded. Some of the material recovered had strange hieroglyphic symbols on it. The townspeople recovered from among the wreckage the body of an 'alien', which they buried in the local cemetery.

Several UFO researchers have tried to uncover some supportive documentation with varying success. Between 1966 and 1977, some went down to Aurora and discovered that a few witnesses were still alive and they confirmed that the story was essentially true. Researchers located the grave where the alien was buried several years ago and tried to get the body exhumed. The request was denied by the authorities.

2 Technology Uncovered

Welcome to Area 51

There is a part of the United States the size of Switzerland that appears blank on every map. It lies in the Nevada desert north-west of Las Vegas. Don't go there. Photography is prohibited and signs warn that it is unlawful to enter the area without permission. Ignore the signs and you will find yourself handcuffed, put in leg irons and strip-searched. Trespassers are known to have been fined $6,000 or jailed for up to a year. And they were the lucky ones. The signs say: 'Use of deadly force authorized.' The airspace over the area is restricted too.

Although nothing is shown on the map, there is plenty there. Along with mountains and creeks, there are roads, buildings, bunkers and a massive runway six miles long. At night the Groom Lake area is a blaze of light. The closed area is known officially as Nellis Air Force Range and Nuclear Test Site. It is home to Area 51. That was a name given to one section of the base on old government maps. And it is generally agreed by UFOlogists that, if the government did have a UFO or a batch of aliens, this is where they would keep it.

The base began in 1954 as a top-secret site where the Lockheed Aircraft Corporation could develop spy planes for the CIA. Since then, the US military's most futuristic technological projects have been developed there. The Stealth bomber and other unconventional aircraft were tested at Nellis. Its very existence has always been shrouded in secrecy. The US Air Force only admitted that Area 51 existed at all in 1994, after Soviet spy satellite footage of the facility was shown in evidence during a court case. The reason for the secrecy, the US government says, is that Nellis is home to the cutting edge of military technology. But the technology is not American. Nor are the technicians working on it. They are from outer space.

Ever since Area 51 was established, it has been the centre of

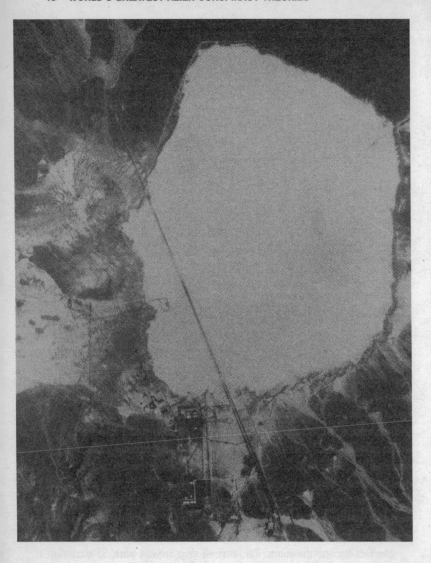

Satellite photograph of Groom Lake area of Area 51, Nevada, USA.

UFO sightings. The authorities issued regular denials. But they found they had egg on their faces when one of their own men said that, not only were there UFOs flying in the airspace above Area 51, but that the USAF was developing alien technology in an underground plant there.

The man's name was Robert 'Bob' Lazar. A child prodigy, he developed a hydrogen-fuelled car and made a jet-powered car and motorbike that had a top speed of 350 miles an hour. At the age of twenty-three, he was employed as a scientist, working on the Strategic Defense Initiative – 'Star Wars' – at the National Laboratory at Los Alamos, New Mexico. Then, in December 1988, he was given a new government contract and sent to work at Area 51. He was shocked and frightened by what he saw and he felt that the American people had a right to know what was going on there. In May 1989, he went on television and revealed that the US government had nine flying saucers in Area 51 and was secretly developing alien technology to its own ends. Knowing the sensitivity of what he was saying, he used the alias 'Dennis'. He was filmed only in silhouette and had his voice electronically distorted. This did no good. Both he and his wife had already received death threats.

After his car was shot at, Lazar realised that he would be safer if he came out into the open and, in November, he gave details of the top-secret 'S4' site, where the alien craft were stored. It was next to Papoose Lake, one of the many dry lakes inside Area 51. An underground complex, it occupied the inside of the whole of Papoose mountain range. Lazar had worked there as part of a team of twenty-two engineers who were employed to work out how the crafts' propulsion systems worked.

Lazar and his colleagues were told little. At first he thought he was working on advanced man-made technology. But when he entered one of the discs, he realised that it was nothing that the Soviets had come up with.

'It has no physical seams, no welds or bolts or rivets,' Lazar said. 'Everything has a soft, round edge to it... as if it's made out of wax and heated for a time and then cooled off.'

Its form and dimensions did not appear to be man-made. Its

Area 51, Nevada: Groom Lake

portholes, arches and tiny chairs were only a foot or so off the ground. Plainly it was designed for creatures a good deal smaller than humans. The propulsion unit, which Lazar and his colleagues worked on, was the size of a baseball. It produced an anti-gravity field which was directed along a hollow column that ran vertically through the centre of the craft. Lazar became convinced it came from another world.

When Lazar got down to work, his suspicions were confirmed. The briefing papers he read were full of UFO information. Among them there were pictures of little grey beings with large hairless heads undergoing autopsies. The briefing papers said the aliens were from the Zeta Reticuli, a star system frequently mentioned as the home of aliens. All this left no doubt in Lazar's mind that he was working with an alien craft built in alien materials by aliens.

Lazar also believes that there were aliens working in S4. One day, as he was passing a room, he saw two men in white lab coats 'looking down and talking to something small with long arms.' He only caught a glimpse. 'I don't know what on earth that was,' said Lazar. But it made sense that it was an alien. And it made sense that it would be kept under lock and key. The briefing papers had mentioned an incident in 1979 where the aliens had killed security guards and scientists at the base.

Although these seem incredible claims, they don't come without corroboration. Since Lazar spilt the beans on TV, over a dozen people have come forward to support his story, though they are afraid of the consequences if they go public. TV journalist George Knapp videotaped one man who ran several large military programmes out at Nellis. He said that the government have had extraterrestrial technology and extraterrestrials themselves since the 1950s. But he will only allow the tape to be screened after his death.

Another journalist tracked down an electrical engineer who had worked at Area 51. He had seen flying saucers there and was willing to say so on TV. But he changed his mind when he found black-suited men parked outside his home day and night. Another witness was threatened more directly. 'We know you do a lot of travelling,' she was told. 'We'd hate an accident to happen to you or your family.'

However, some witnesses have been prepared to talk outside the United States. In 1995, a German film company released a video called *Secrets of the Black World*. In it, a number of witnesses give testimonies that support Lazar's story and prove that something is going on in Area 51. Even more fantastically, the video includes a clip of grainy film, shot inside S4, showing a roomful of canisters where the bodies of dead aliens were stored.

The video also shows UFOs being tested over the base. This was confirmed by the dogged Norio Hayakawa of Nippon TV who camped out outside Area 51 for nights on end. Eventually his patience was rewarded. He caught a fleeting glimpse of a mysterious light rising from the base and filmed a glowing object as it disappeared over the mountains. 'It seemed to "skate" through the sky,' he said. State-of-the-art computer analysis of Hayakawa's film has shown that the object was 'definitely no conventional aircraft'.

Other films shot in the area show the same thing – a bright object that hopped through the sky at incredible speeds and performed impossible manoeuvres. One of these objects actually buzzed an NBC-TV crew, leaving them with radiation burns.

On 28 February 1990, UFO researcher Billy Goodman photographed another UFO over Groom Lake, where it was thought that alien craft were being tested. Freedom Heights, which overlooks Groom Lake's six-mile runway, has been off-limits to the public since April 1995. The idea that something unworldly is going on there has also percolated into the public consciousness. Highway 375, which runs past Groom Lake, was renamed 'Extraterrestrial Highway' in 1996.

There is no doubt that something strange is going on in the Nevada desert. In 1987, Robert Frost, a worker at Area 51, came home screaming in pain and fear. His symptoms were attributed to a mysterious chemical fire, but he was dead two years later. Other victims sued. It was this case that forced the USAF to finally admit that Area 51 existed.

According to aviation journalist Jim Goodall, there are at least eight 'black programs' flying out of Area 51. These black programs are ultra-secret government projects that cost the American taxpayer $35 billion a year. According to those in the industry, they include the production of fast and highly manoeuvrable unmanned probes that could easily be mistaken for flying saucers.

But Goodall believes there is more to it. Reliable witnesses have seen some of these silent and incredibly fast craft. One flew out of Area 51 and was later tracked by the Federal Aviation Administration Center travelling at over ten thousand miles an hour. That is some thirteen times the speed of sound, well beyond the capability of any known human technology.

Former President of Lockheed Advance Development Ben Rich told Goodall that he was a 'firm believer' in UFOs. Goodall also tracked an ex-Lockheed worker who said, 'We have things flying in the Nevada desert that would make [*Star Wars* director] George Lucas drool.'

Many dismiss such statements as government-orchestrated dis-information designed to cover-up what really is going on. Naturally there has been a well-organised campaign to discredit Lazar. This is led by the physicist and UFOlogist Stanton Friedman, who does not believe that Lazar worked at Area 51. Nor does he believe that Lazar has the scientific credentials he claims.

'Not one shred of evidence has been put forward to support this great story,' says Friedman. 'No diplomas, resumes, transcripts, or memberships of professional organisations.'

Lazar claims to have Masters degrees from the California Institute of Technology and the Massachusetts Institute of Technology. Friedman says that they can find no record of him. What's more, he doubts Lazar's practical background.

'Bob is not a scientist,' says Friedman. 'He failed to answer all scientific questions put to him.'

The US government deny that Lazar worked at Los Alamos from 1982 to 1984, as he claimed. But when George Knapp checked this out, he found Lazar's name in the internal phone directory at Los Alamos. Strangely, the government never denied that Lazar worked in Area 51 – and a salary statement was issued by the US Department of Naval Intelligence.

Lazar's motives have also been questioned. He has sold the movie rights to his story and his drawings of the extraterrestrial ship have been used to merchandise a model of the craft. He made the story up, it is implied, to make money. But Lazar is clear that he went public because the secrecy surrounding the activities at Area 51 is an insult to science and to the American people. However, since he lost his job at Area 51, he has had money trou-bles. A divorce in 1990 left him bankrupt and, in April 1990, he was arrested for his business links with a Las Vegas brothel. He was sentenced to six months probation and 150 hours community service.

But on camera, Lazar is a convincing witness. He is cool, calm and unpretentious. He has always told the same story – something unusual among fantasists and false witnesses. And he claims no expertise in fields where he has none. One particularly convincing detail that surfaced in his televised testimony is that Lazar said workers at S4 wore badges carrying the letters MAJ. This plainly refers to Majestic-12, a top-secret flying saucer research group set up by the President Truman in 1947.

What's more, those in a position to know agree with him. Dr Edgar Mitchell, the sixth astronaut to walk on the moon and founder of the Institute of Noetic Studies, a think-tank, said: 'There is strong evidence that a covert group within the US government is engaged in the back-engineering of alien spacecraft.'

And he is concerned about how things are going.

'I am extremely worried this is no longer a government operation, but one run by private parties that are unaccountable – and use billions of dollars in black budget funds.'

Landing at Area 51

One of the most intriguing UFO reports to have surfaced over the years is a report of a crash – or perhaps a landing – that occurred in Nellis, Nevada in 1962. For many years this case was thought of as nothing more than a rumour amongst UFO researchers. However, reports and statements from many eyewitnesses slowly emerged, and there was enough for researchers to start digging for more information.

The object was first spotted over Oneida, New York, and was heading in a westerly direction. There were also reports of the object in Kansas, Colorado and Eureka, Utah. The object was then seen over Reno, Nevada, and was seen to turn and head towards Las Vegas. On the way it disappeared into Nellis. The object was also tracked at several radar sites.

The object was reported by over a thousand people, most of whom assumed that the object was a meteorite. Various newspapers covered the story the following morning, although most of them concluded also that it must have been just a very spectacular meteorite. The object was also seen at various times by several commercial airline pilots who reported that the object was below them, which is unusual for a meteorite. And the Air Defence Command, after watching the object for several hours, scrambled several fighters – not something that they normally do for meteorites.

More remarkably, on its way to Nellis, the object seems to have touched down near Eureka at the same time as the town experienced a total blackout. When it took off again, the power came back.

The official USAF explanation was that it was a meteorite. However, this does not explain why fighters were scrambled, how it changed direction or why the object appeared to land and then take off again.

Sudden Breakthroughs

In 1947, Major Philip J. Corso had seen the corpse of a dead alien. It was one of the creatures that had been killed in the crash at Roswell on 2 July. The alien had been in a wooden crate, one among some thirty stored in a US Army warehouse. Fourteen years later he was to come across those crates again.

By 1961, Philip J. Corso had risen to the rank of Lieutenant Colonel. He had been posted to the Pentagon, where he was in charge of the Foreign Technology desk in the US Army's Research and Development Division. His job was to evaluate enemy weapons systems and other foreign technology. Typically his work involved stripping down captured Soviet MiGs to find out why they were so much better than American fighter planes.

In 1961, Corso's commanding officer and close friend General Arthur Trudeau offered him a top-secret assignment. Corso was to report on the contents of a number of crates. They turned out to be the same crates he had seen in the warehouse fourteen years before.

The crates were wheeled into his office. Then he locked the room and started to open them. He was relieved to find there were no bodies in them this time. However, what he did find was just as mysterious – or so it seemed at the time.

He found a set of strange filaments that were clear and flexible, and made of something like glass – though he had never seen glass that bent before. As he examined them, he noticed that when he pointed a strand towards a source of light, the other end lit up. The filaments seemed to conduct light along their length. Next he came across wafer-thin squares of material. They appeared to be made from some form of plastic and were covered in tiny intricate patterns that had somehow been etched into their surface. After studying the squares for some time, Corso realised that he was looking at some form of electrical circuit, like that on a printed circuit board. But this circuitry was far more intricate and there were no holes where electronic components could be soldered in position.

Then he found some dull, greyish, fibrous material, which resembled aluminium foil. But Corso found he could not tear the material. Nor could he fold or bend it. Whatever he did to it, it simply sprang back to its original shape. It was exhibiting a physical property that would later be called 'supertenacity'. This property is well known now, but it was unheard of in 1961.

A file had come with the crates and Corso sat down to read it. It said that a set of dark, elliptical eyepieces had been found attached to a creature that had been found in a crashed UFO. They were as thin as human skin but exhibited the magic property of illuminating images in low-light conditions, allowing the wearer to see in the dark.

In the file, he also came across a description of a device that contained a power source and looked like a stubby torch. But the beam it produced was so intense that it could burn its way through solid material. When Corso read later about bizarre cattle mutilations associated with UFOs, it seemed to him that this device had been used on the unfortunate livestock – it was plainly a surgical cutting tool.

The growing incidence of cattle mutilations formed a vital part of the conclusion of Corso's chilling report to General Trudeau. From what he had seen, Corso deduced that the aliens in the crashed UFO were genetically altered humanoids. They were cloned biological entities who were harvesting biological material on Earth for their own experimentation. Their technology was clearly superior to our own and they were a clear danger to humankind. The American government had only one option: it had to prepare for a possible conflict. Corso's recommendation was that they begin 'reverse-engineering' – that is attempting to re-create the alien technology recovered at the crash site in order to find out how it worked. General Trudeau accepted Corso's report and endorsed his plan, but they had to find trustworthy scientists and technicians to carry out the work.

The Cold War was at its peak in the early 1960s, and secrecy was paramount for the US military. However, the McCarthy hearings of the 1950s and the investigations of the House Un-American Activities Committee had convinced Trudeau and Corso that the military was too full of leaks to be given the job of back-engineering the alien technology. The last thing they needed was for the Soviets to get hold of it. Trudeau said that the only people they could trust were themselves. So they labelled the alien artefacts as 'foreign technology' and treated them as if they were parts of a captured Soviet MiG fighter.

'Foreign technology was the absolute perfect cover,' said Corso. 'All I had to do was figure out what to do with the stuff I had.'

Trudeau and Corso had access to the most eminent army scientists of their day but, more than anything, they feared that the security of their project would be compromised. Scientists talked to each other and were likely to put two and two together. Instead, they decided to farm the alien devices out to various trusted figures in the business world. Commercial companies rarely talk to each other and have every reason to guard their secrets. Over the next two years, Corso delivered the aliens' devices to the research divisions of many defence contractors, including leading engineering and telecommunications firms. The army funded the back-engineering by paying 'research costs', while the companies benefited by filing patents on their 'discoveries'.

UFOlogist Stanton Friedman goes along with this theory, though he believes that the programme began before Corso got his hands on the contents of the crates.

'An example would be the transistor by Bell Labs,' he says. 'Bell has close ties with Scandia National Laboratory in Albuquerque – one of the trio of high-security US nuclear weapons manufacturers. The official birthday of the transistor is given as 23

December 1947 – six months after Roswell.'

Throughout the 1960s, these companies claimed responsibility for a number of 'miracle breakthroughs' – fibre optics, integrated circuit chips, night-vision goggles, lasers and supertenacity fibres –all of which had come from Corso's crates. Once US companies had perfected the technology, it became part of the arsenal of the US military. The 'seeding' of these new super-technologies has also spawned numerous civilian applications. Anyone that has used a CD player, operated a modern computer or made a transatlantic phone call has been benefiting from alien technology.

Dulce, New Mexico

Area 51 in the deserts of Nevada is not the only place where aliens are assisting the American military with their technology. There is another secret base in the north of New Mexico, near the town of Dulce and close to the Jicarilla Indian Reservation. Dulce has a population of just nine hundred. It is an out-of-the-way and other-wise unremarkable place. However, UFO researchers have discovered that it is home to the most incredible and sinister facility. Under the desert plains nearby is a secret underground base. The vast complex is home to a joint US government–alien biogenetic laboratory, which carries out hideous experiments on both humans and animals.

The base came to light when Security Officer Thomas Edwin Castello spilled the beans in a document known as *The Dulce Papers*, which he circulated in the early 1980s. By then the project had been going on for a considerable time. Castello had taken the documents from the Dulce underground facility, and he backed them with a videotape and over thirty black-and-white photographs. He had worked as a security officer at the Dulce base until 1979, but by then he had had his fill of what was going on in the complex and decided to part company with his secretive employers. But before he left, he stole some documents and removed a security videotape which showed various views of the underground complex from the base's control centre. He made five copies of the documents, and hid the originals. The copies were then distributed to the UFO community via intermediaries.

Realising that what he had seen at the base was extremely sensitive, he knew that he and his family would be in danger. They had to go into hiding. But when he went to pick up his wife and children, government agents were waiting for him. He fled and never saw his family again.

Castello was in his mid-twenties when he first joined the service and was given training in photography at a top-secret underground facility in West Virginia. He stayed with the US Air Force for seven years, leaving in 1971 to work for the Rand Corporation – America's military think -tank – in Santa Monica, California. By 1977, he was considered trustworthy and he was transferred to the secret Dulce facility. He bought a home in Santa Fe, and commuted to work from there five days a week via a shuttle system that ran deep underground. In the hallway of the tube stations hallway, he saw a sign that read: 'To Los Alamos'. The tracks, he believes, also led on to the underground base in the Nevada desert that is known as Area 51.

The work force at Dulce was strange, to say the least. Castello estimates that there were over 18,000 small 'Grey' aliens on staff, along with hundreds of reptilian humanoids known as the 'Draco'. The underground facility was so large that it had seven sub-levels. The aliens lived on level five and worked on levels six and seven.

All sorts of bizarre experiments were going on there. The aliens were doing research into hypnosis, telepathy and dreams. Another area of interest was human auras. This had paid dividends, Castello said. The aliens were able to separate the 'bioplasmic body from the physical body', and place an 'alien life-force' within a human body after removing the human's 'soul'.

Level six of the complex was known as 'Nightmare Hall'. This was where the aliens did hideous genetic experiments on all forms of terrestrial life – fish, seals, mice, birds and, of course, humans. There was a storage area for the results of these experiments. Tanks contained multi-armed and multi-legged humans, while cages housed tall, humanoid, bat-like creatures. There were 'row upon row of thousands of humans, human-mixture remains and embryos of humanoids kept in cold storage,' Castello says.

But worst: 'I frequently encountered humans in cages. Usually they were dazed or drugged, but sometimes they cried and begged for help. We were told that they were hopelessly insane, and involved in high-risk drug tests to cure insanity. We were told never to speak to them at all.'

Despite these grisly experiments, it seemed that the aliens had no hostile intentions. Both the Greys and the reptilian aliens seemed to have been on Earth for thousands of years. Humans didn't bother them. They were far more concerned about other space-faring races. The aliens didn't seem to be interested in the land, minerals, fuel or water that Earth could offer them either. Their primary concern was the magnetic power of the Earth. The aliens have learnt to harvest this energy in a way unknown to terrestrial science. Magnetic energy was used to control the elevators and supply heat and power to the base.

The Dulce Papers show that the aliens were working hand in hand with the US government. Castello can reel off a list of US government agencies who maintained a presence at Dulce. They included the Department of Energy, the National Institute of Health, the National Science Foundation, the Howard Hughes Medical Institute and the Department of the Environment. Castello himself was recruited through his government service.

Security was super-tight at the Dulce facility. Visitors were weighed, naked, before being allowed to enter. Their weight was recorded, then they were given a one-piece suit and an ID card that could be used to access the various level. There were scales scattered throughout the complex. Everyone's weight was recorded every day and a gain of more than three pounds would lead to a thorough physical examination, including an X-ray. Everyone who worked there was under the surveillance of the security guards at all times. No one was allowed to carry anything into sensitive areas. Everything was delivered by conveyor belt and X-rayed before being distributed.

Since Thomas Castello went public with his story, he has become a regular speaker at a number of UFO conventions.

Although he comes over as a highly plausible witness, some have chosen to dismiss his accounts. But it has not derailed Castello, who says that there are other alien bases scattered throughout the solar systems. There are similar facilities on the moons of Saturn and Jupiter.

Along with the photographic and documentary evidence Castello has presented, circumstantial evidence that something strange is going on at Dulce had been accruing. Between 1976 and 1978, Dulce was the centre of a string of cattle mutilations that left local ranchers mystified. Senseless and unexplainable attacks on livestock became so frequent that research teams from all over the world converged on the tiny town. In July 1978, scientist Howard Burgess discovered that many Dulce cattle were covered with strange markings that only showed up when they were placed under ultra-violet light. A glittery substance was found on the right side of their necks, on the right ear and on the right leg. Analysis of the substance revealed that is was rich in magnesium and potassium. Dulce is also a Mecca for UFO sightings, many of which occurred around the same time the mutilated cows were found. And following up on Castello's story, a research team took soundings of the ground in the area. It revealed a complex of deep cavities under the mesa.

Naturally, the US government refuses to acknowledge the existence of any military installation around or under Dulce, New Mexico – just as they denied the existence of Area 51. However, they will have to pit their wits against legions of UFO researchers determined to unearth the town's dark secret.

Bugging Dulce

One UFO researcher, Paul Bennewitz, claimed some success in finding out what was going on in the base at Dulce. Not only did he photograph UFOs over Dulce, he made contact with the aliens in the facility. After two years of tracking the craft, he managed to establish constant video reception from the alien motherships and their underground base. And he could communicate with them via computer using hexadecimal code. Subsequent photographs he received showed landing pylons and ships on the ground, along with aliens on the ground riding around in vehicles powered by static electricity. They also used static electricity to charge their beam weapons.

His constant interaction with the aliens gave him a clear picture of alien psychology. Although he never met them directly, he understood their logic and ways of thinking and got an insight into their intentions. Every night, he discovered, they were abducting people, cutting them and implanting devices into them, though he is not sure that the implants are totally effective. However, he estimates that over 300,000 people have been implanted in the US and over two million world-wide.

Then things began to go wrong. In 1985, he suffered a nervous breakdown. According to colleagues, this was cause by a government disinformation campaign designed to subvert his activities and ruin his reputation. It succeeded.

What UFOs Can Teach Us

There is nothing intrinsically wrong with what is going on in Area 51. Humankind has every reason to try and learn from aliens and alien technology. After all, they are plainly much more advanced than we are. Simply look at the astonishing flight characteristics of UFOs: they can accelerate instantly to enormous speeds – measured at over 10,000 miles an hour – then come instantly to a halt. They can do high-speed right-angle turns without slowing, or hover motionless in the sky with no visible means of support. Clearly they do not operate on the same principles as a conventional aircraft. Indeed, they seem to violate the laws of physics at will.

Even to reach the solar system from a distant star system in a reasonable length of time means that they would have to travel faster than the speed of light. This is one reason why many scientists choose to dismiss the subject of UFOs altogether. However, it is a violation of the principles of science itself to ignore observations that are in favour of an established theory. It is a fundamental principle that laws of physics should be modified to reflect the data, not vice versa.

With this philosophy in mind, a handful of scientists have tried to explain the extraordinary behaviour of UFOs using the normal laws of physics to see what advances can be made. By studying the thousands of detailed reports that have been provided by credible witnesses, they have attempted to discover the science and technology utilised by alien spacecraft. Leader in the field is physicist Paul Hill, who worked with NASA for twenty-five years.

Hill set to work on the most credible reports from the 1950s, 1960s and 1970s. He avoided the fruitless speculation about whether UFOs are real or not, and accepted the reports at face value and analysed them as he would any other scientific data. His first conclusion was that UFOs do not defy the laws of physics. This finding has subsequently been confirmed by scientists working in a new field of physics called 'breakthrough propulsion'. Their aim is to develop propellantless propulsion systems. The result would be craft that emulate the flight characteristics of UFOs.

To appreciate how radical UFO propulsion systems are, you need to understand how conventional aircraft work. An engine is bolted to an airframe. This engine produces thrust which pushes the aircraft and pilot forward. According to Newton's first law of motion, a body continues in a uniform state of motion – that is, travelling at a constant speed in a straight line – until a force acts on it. This gives rise to the concept of inertia, the property of matter that resists charges in speed or direction. When an aircraft makes a turn, say, the atoms of the plane and the pilot want to continue in a straight path. To overcome their inertia, a force must be applied. This is provided by banking the plane so that the lift provided by the wings, instead of pushing directly upwards, is angled and pushes the plane around the turn.

Newton's third law of motion states that, for every action there is an equal and opposite reaction. So when the air under the wings pushes the plane around the turn, the wings push on the air with an equal and opposite force. This force is felt by the pilot as the G-force that pushes him down in his seat. The faster or more violent the turn, the higher G-force created. Even high-speed manoeuvres in a plane can produce G-forces that will result in the unconsciousness or death of the pilot. G-force can even tear the airframe apart. Hill has calculated that UFOs regularly pull an astonishing 100 G. This is more than enough to kill any human being and tear apart any plane that has been built. The question is, how do UFOs overcome the effects of inertia?

Hill has an answer. A UFO would have to generate a force field to power and steer the craft. In conventional physics, only three such force fields have been discovered outside the atomic – electric, magnetic and gravitational. So which are UFOs using?

To answer that question, Hill again turns back to eyewitness testimony. One case provides a clue. A farmer in Missouri was confronted by a flying saucer, fifteen feet in diameter, hovering just above the ground. In an attempt to scare it off, the intrepid soul threw a rock at it. But instead of clunking into the structure of the craft, the man observed the rock bounce off an invisible force field some fifteen feet from the hull itself. From this, Hill concludes that the field is gravitational – electric or magnetic fields would have no effect on a non-magnetic substance such as rock.

Somehow UFOs generate a localised repulsive force field. This could be characterised as an anti-gravitational field or negative gravity. A craft that could generate anti-gravity could counteract the attractive force of Earth's gravity. It could hover or fly vertically into the sky at will. And, by angling the anti-gravity field, it could produce thrust in any direction. Flying saucers are not usually seen to have external propulsion components. This would account for that. The anti-gravity field produced by a propulsion unit inside the craft would have permeated the hull without affecting it. That means that the hull would be impervious to gravity, thus it would be effectively weightless. It would also have no inertia. It is also a basic law of physics that gravitational fields travel at the speed of light. This would mean that the craft would have limitless acceleration and deceleration, and incredible speed.

Although all this sounds inconceivable, there is nothing new about the idea. It was first proposed by Professor Hermann Oberth, the father of Germany's wartime rocket programme, who, after World War II, headed the US government commission on UFOs. 'UFOs are directed by intelligent beings of a very high order, and are propelled by distorting the gravitational field, converting gravity into usable energy,' he said.

But Hill has worked this out in more detail and, theoretically at least, discovered how an anti-gravity field could be used to rid the craft and those inside it of inertia. As well as directing the field outside the craft for thrust and manoeuvring, the field would also envelop the physical mass of the ship and, for that matter, the atmosphere surrounding it. The force is generated uniformly around the craft, and does not originate from a single point such as a jet or rocket; the ship effectively becomes its own centre of gravity. So if the field wants the craft to make a right turn, then all the atoms on or in the craft and the occupants, would turn together. There would be no G-forces caused by one part pushing on another. It would be as effortless as falling down a lift-shaft. Effectively there would be no inertia. Such a means of propulsion would explain all of the observations of UFO activity that have so puzzled scientists.

The fact that the anti-gravity field also acts on the atmosphere surrounding the UFO would explain why UFOs – unless they are crippled and about to crash – are able to exceed the speed of sound without creating sonic booms. In a conventional aircraft, the air in front of its surfaces has to be pushed out of the way. But the fastest air can move, normally, is the speed of sound. Consequently, as the aircraft's speed increases, air builds up in front of it. When the plane reaches the speed of sound, it is facing a solid wall of air. If the speed is increased, this wall of air is blasted apart, producing a shock wave, or sonic boom. Using wind-tunnel studies and computer simulation, Hill has shown that supersonic flight can easily be achieved by UFOs without sonic booms. All it has to do is use its force field to keep the airflow around the craft at subsonic speeds. No matter how fast the ship is travelling, the airflow over its surfaces remains the same.

Another advantage of this is that small objects such dust, rain and insects would not hit the hull of the craft, causing damage. It would also explain how UFOs avoid burning up from enormous heat caused by air friction when flying at enormous speeds and why they have been observed to emerge from the sea without getting wet.

Key to manoeuvring a UFO is the ability to direct the force field. Hill notes that witnesses often report that discs tilt down when moving forward and tilt up when stopping. They also exhibit a characteristic 'falling leaf' wobble when descending. Using advanced mathematics, Hill has been able to show that these are exactly the movements that would be produced if some kind of repulsive force field was being used. Hill also has a theory on what sort of mechanism is used to guide this field energy.

'In a saucer, the power focusing or driving link, is comprised of a bladed mechanism located in the ringed area just within and below the rim,' he says. He bases this on a series of close-up observations made by witnesses who saw movable plates in UFOs shortly before they took off.

One of those accounts came from Ray Hawks. On 11 August 1960, he saw a strange craft drop vertically out of a cloud over Boulder, Colorado, and hover about a hundred feet above the ground. It looked like two convex discs joined at the perimeter. Hawks says it was dull grey in colour. A little way from the rim, he saw a series of shiny plates. These were separated by small radial gaps. They appeared both on the underside, which he could see quite clearly, and on the upper surface, which came into view as the craft wobbled to a halt. One of the plates was giving off blue smoke, but it tilted, retracted inside the craft and was replaced by another one, which gave off a click as it fell into place. The craft then shot off back into the clouds.

A similar sighting was made on 2 March 1965, in Weeki Wachee Springs, Florida, when John Reeves came upon a flying saucer in a clearing in a wood. It was above twenty to thirty feet in diameter and sat on four legs. He managed to get within a hundred feet of it and saw around the rim of the saucer a series of blades. These were standing out so that he could see through them and into the saucer itself. After a short time, the blades closed, the rim began to rotate and the UFO lifted off into the air.

Developing a gravity field such as those used by UFOs is well beyond our current technological capabilities. Indeed, there is no single theory within the known laws of physics that can explain how a field propulsion system that nullifies or manipulates gravity would work. However, there are two main schools of thought. One operates within Einstein's space-time theories. It speculates that the gravity field produced by UFOs warps the fabric of space-time and allows the craft to travel along the contours of warped space without incurring inertia.

The other falls into the realms of the as-yet incomplete Grand Unified Theory, which is attempting to unify the four known forces that regulate the universe – the nuclear strong force, nuclear weak force, electromagnetic force and gravity. Gravity is unique among all the forces as it has no known opposing force; it only attracts and does not repel.

The Grand Unified Theory postulates that the four forces of the universe are in some way related. This has led some physicists to speculate that UFO propulsion systems somehow harness the electromagnetic force, say in such a way that gravity is neutralised or redirected. It would work by generating a continuous stream of antigravitons – antiparticles of gravity. These would bounce back and forth between the craft and the source of the gravitational field affecting it, and nullify its gravitational force.

Hill rules out the possibility of the field being electromagnetic in nature, but he admits the possibility that electromagnetic forces could be used to generate such a field, in a way that is currently not understood. UFOs sightings often report effects similar to those produced by large electromagnetic fields – and interference with electrical systems, car engines cutting out, guidance computers on aircraft failing. Even the chemical changes found in soil where UFOs have landed could be caused by microwave radiation.

This would also explain why UFOs are often invisible to radar. If the electromagnetic field operating the anti-gravity propulsion system was sufficiently strong in the microwave section of the spectrum it would simply absorb incoming radar waves. This was confirmed by a USAF electronic countermeasure plane that was tailed by a UFO. The onboard equipment measured the UFO's microwave output at over one megawatt.

Some faltering steps have already been made in the field of antigravity. In the 1950s, American scientist T. Townsend Brown worked on electromagnetically induced antigravity, or electrogravitics. He built a disc-shaped capacitor that exhibited a propulsive force in the direction of the positive electrode. The higher the charge, the greater the electrogravitic force. Using a charge of several hundred thousand volts, he could fire a three-foot disc at speeds of several hundreds of miles an hour.

And in 1992, at Tempere University in Finland, two physicists – R. Nieminen and E. Podkletnov – tried a different approach when they noticed strange antigravitational effects on smoke when it moved up a column above a series of rapidly rotating superconducting ceramic discs. Small weights suspended on a strain gauge above this contraption showed a weight loss of two per cent.

It seems that human technology is just not up to the task yet. So if propellantless propulsion has been developed already – and sightings at Area 51 show it has – it would have to be back-engineering from crashed or captured alien technology. In that case, it would be of paramount economic importance to keep its development totally secret. Introducing a propulsion system that was much more efficient than jets or rockets and does without chemical or fossil fuels would have a devastating effect on the global economy.

Nevertheless, there is talk in the scientific community of 'breakthrough propulsion physics'. If UFO-style propulsion was introduced in ten or twenty years, the world economy would have time to adjust.

Secrets of the Nazi Saucers

The American scientists at Area 51 are not the first to work on flying saucers. It seems that German scientists were well down that track towards the end of World War II.

At that time the Third Reich's aeronautical engineers were far ahead of those of the Allies, who had invested most of their technical expertise in developing the atomic bomb. In the dying days of the war, Hitler had an extraordinary array of 'Vengeance' weapons, with which he hoped to reverse the course of the war. Only two of them, the V-1 pilotless aircraft and the V-2 ballistic missile, were actually used.

But by 1945, German engineers had developed over 130 types of rockets and missiles. The ME-110 jet fighter was equipped to carry twenty-four air-to-air missiles and the prototype of a jet-powered flying wing was being built by Walter and Reimar Horten. Even more futuristic was the delta-shaped Horten DM-1, which some have compared to the B2 Stealth bomber.

But that was not the half of it. When the Third Reich was finally overrun and its secret weapons bases captured, the Allies realised how sophisticated some of Hitler's terror weapons were. Among the discoveries in a research facility deep underground was the existence of a programme to build a disc-shaped flying craft, the V-7 – the Nazis' own flying saucer.

As with other German research programmes, the technology and the personnel were co-opted into secret Allied projects at the end of the war. Some researchers believe that the V-7 project provided the technology for America to develop its own man-made UFO.

Even after all these years, it is difficult to make out what exactly was going on in Germany's underground bunkers. The Germans destroyed many of their underground bases as they retreated, and anything captured by Allied troops was immediately classified. However, some of those who worked on the V-7 and other top-secret projects have come forward to reveal what they knew about Germany's flying saucers.

In the spring of 1941, Luftwaffe aeronautical engineer Dr Rudolf Schriever designed a prototype disc-shaped craft called 'The Flying Top'. Schriever later collaborated with two other German engineers, Habermohl and Miethe, and an Italian named Giuseppe Belluzzo. However, Belluzzo claimed that he was the one who came up with the idea for a man-made 'flying saucer' and the idea was later taken up by the Germans.

Whoever first thought of it, it is generally agreed that Schriever, Habermohl, Miethe and Belluzzo designed a series of flying discs for the Nazis and the first prototype was ready for test flights in June 1942. The first models were powered by gas turbines. Later the craft were modified to make use of the new advanced jet engines that the Nazis had developed. Schriever and Habermohl's design for a jet-powered disc showed a fixed, cupola-style cockpit with a wide-surface ring rotating around it. This ring incorporated movable wing surfaces that could be reconfigured for take-off, landing and level flight.

Blueprints of Schriever's disc have been declassified, but many UFO researchers claim that they have been doctored. Even so, the designs show a fifty-foot diameter disc that sits on four legs. This concept was very advanced for the time, but is now familiar from UFO sightings. Although the details are missing from the plans, the craft was said to have been equipped with radar, lasers and 'electromagnetic turbines' – possibly of the type Paul Hill speculates about.

Another disc-shaped craft was designed by Dr Miethe. It was an amazing 140 feet in diameter and powered by jets with swivelling nozzles, later seen on the Harrier jump jet. The craft had phenomenal performance, reaching speeds of nearly 1,250 miles an hour and climbing over 32,000 feet in under three minutes, easily outperforming any aircraft of its time. Miethe's saucer made a test flight on 14 February 1945. It was only when a design finally became operational that it acquired its V number. Miethe's craft became V-7. Interestingly, Miethe's disc had twin cockpits above and below the body of the disc and twin jet pipes at the rear. Its design is strikingly similar to the B2 Stealth bomber.

If Miethe's designs have been recycled in the Stealth programme, how much else of the flying saucer technology developed by the Germans during World War II has surfaced in top-secret American projects? Rudolf Schriever, for one, believes that a lot of it found its way into use. Much of the UFO activity reported after the war, he believes, were sightings of craft built by the Americans from his designs.

It is known that Miethe was recruited by the Allies to continue the work he had done earlier in Germany, just as Werner von Braun, designer of the V-2, was recruited by the Americans to work on the rocket programme. Henry Stevens, head of a research group devoted to exploring the Nazi disc programme, unearthed a declassified US project from 1955 to build a jet-powered saucer capable of reaching Mach 3.4 (3.4 times the speed of sound) at 80,000 feet. It was to be built by a Canadian company called A.V. Roe. Stevens found that one 'Miethe – Designer 1950' was listed on their personnel roster.

There was also the *Feuerball* – or 'fireball' – project unearthed by Dr Renato Vesco. This was a sophisticated, radio-controlled anti-aircraft weapon that was able to jam enemy radar and attack enemy aircraft using a 'multi-batteried blower cannon'. A flat disc, it was powered by a special turbojet engine that was developed by scientists at the aeronautical establishment in Wiener Neustadt. It actually saw action towards the end of the war when one was seen to attack a squadron of American Liberator bombers. One burst into flames after the *Feuerball* 'emitted a bluish cloud of smoke'. According to Vesco, the principles of the *Feuerball* were used to develop a larger supersonic craft called the *Kugelblitz*, or 'ball lightning' fighter, at the underground facilities at Kahla, in Thuringia, central Germany. The *Kugelblitz* took to the air in February 1945, three months before the end of the war in Europe.

A mysterious aspect of the V-7 weapons' story is the involvement of the Thule Society – an occult group that restricted its membership to high-ranking German Army officers and the professional classes. It perpetuated German racial myths and provided Hitler with much of his Nazi ideology. Even the Swastika was originally the symbol of the Thule group.

The Thule Society, which even claimed kinship to a race of alien beings who lived inside the earth, were said to have mastered a new form of energy, called 'Vril'. American UFOlogist Colonel Wendelle Stevens says that the breakthrough was made at the University of Vienna before the war. A group that called itself the Vril Society found ways to manipulate forces underlying the physical universe. This knowledge was later combined with other new energy technologies. It seems to have influenced the work of Victor Schauberger, an Austrian who invented machines operated by 'inward spiralling' – power was generated from implosion, rather than explosions as in the internal combustion engine.

Schauberger applied the principle 'understand nature, then copy nature' to all his work. After observing the spiralling motion of water, he developed the concept of an engine powered by implosion. His theory was: 'If water or air is rotated into a twisting form known as a "colloidal", a build up of energy results, which, with immense power, can cause levitation.' When the Nazis took over Austria in 1938 Schauberger was arrested and, with his family under threat of execution, he worked on his energy-generating device for the Germans. He developed a flying disc for the Nazis and used 'liquid vortex propulsion', a technology that nullified gravity. It was test flown, but both the prototype and his plans were destroyed by the retreating Nazis. Schauberger was taken to America, where he worked on a secret project for the US government. An oath of secrecy he signed prevented him from ever writing or talking about his inventions. On his deathbed, he said: 'They have stolen everything from me, everything. I don't even own myself.'

The Vril Society also experimented with other exotic technology. These included a device, designed by Hans Kohler, which was called the Kohler tachyon magneto-gravitic drive, or, alternatively, the Thule tachyonator. Wendelle Stevens says that these exotic devices developed under the auspices of the Vril Society were used to construct the so-called Vril discs. These were highly advanced flying discs that were thirty foot in diameter and designed to be used as fighter interceptors. Stevens claims that the electromagnetic field propulsion technology they used was later incorporated into the seventy-five foot diameter Haunebu discs that were successfully tested in 1941. Haunebu discs, he says, were used to attack and destroy Allied bombers attacking the ball-bearing factories at Schweinfurth in 1943. SS blueprints and photographs of the Vril and Haunebu discs were published in Germany in the book *Die*

Dunkle Seite des Mondes ('The dark Side of the Moon') by Brad Harris.

Although the Vril craft did not tip World War II in favour of the Nazis, there are suggestions that the technology was spirited away before the fall of Berlin to await the call of the Reich at some future time. According to author W.A. Harbinson, under the influence of the Thule Society, Hitler began seeking a foothold in Antarctica. In 1938 German expeditions mapped an area of Queen Maud Land, the area of the Antarctic directly south of Africa. Although the plateau there is covered by an ice sheet up to one-and-a-half miles thick, there were several sections free of ice where rocky peaks pierce the ice caps. The Nazis was renamed it Neu-Schwabenland. Throughout the war, the Nazis ferried materiel there to build a huge underground base. Once it was complete, the Vril discs were secretly installed.

In 1947, the US Navy carried out a huge exercise called Operation Highjump off Neu-Schwabenland. According to Harbinson, the exercise was a cover for an operation to root out any Nazis surviving in the secret base. It ended badly for the Americans when they encountered Germans armed with flying Vril disc technology. The US had no weapons that could match them and were forced to withdraw. After this defeat, the US pulled out of the Antarctic for a decade and began to develop its own disc techno logy, based on what they had managed to salvage from the Nazi facilities they had overrun. So America had every reason to continue the work begun by Schriever, Miethe, Habermohl, Belluzzo, Schauberger and others, and develop their own V-7.

3 Animal Mutilations

The Slaughter Begins

Alien abductions have been closely associated with the disturbing phenomenon of animal mutilations. They began in the 1960s. The victim of the first documented case concerned a young horse called Lady, who was being raised on a farm near Alamosa in the San Luis Valley, Colorado. Every night she would turn up at the ranch house for her food and water. Then on 8 September 1967, for the first time, she did not show up.

The next day, Lady's owner Berle Lewis went out to try and find the horse. He found her dead with her flesh stripped from the neck upwards. The case was so unusual that a pathology examination was ordered. The pathologist Dr John Altshuler was shocked to

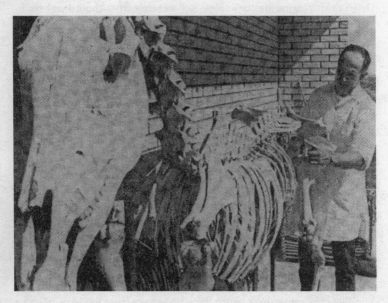

The skeleton of the horse Lady, on display in Alamosa, Colorado, with vet Dr Wallace A. Leary.

find that Lady's brain, spine and internal organs, including the heart, had been removed with incredible precision. Some of the cuts were as clean as a surgeon's scalpel. It was a professional job. Even more baffling was that the mare's body had been completely drained of blood without so much as a stain on or around the corpse. Dr Altshuler also took tissue samples. When he examined them under a microscope, he found even more disturbing evidence.

'There was a darkened colour as if the flesh had been opened and cauterised with a surgical cauterising blade,' he said later, 'almost as if it had been done with a modern-day laser.'

Although lasers had first been developed in the early 1960s, surgical laser technology capable of causing such wounds was not available in 1967. The possibilities of the technology were widely known, but what lasers there were, were vastly expensive research tools confined to university and industrial laboratories. They were not the sort of thing you toted about on the prairies of Colorado.

Several explanations were given, ranging from the horse being struck by a bolt of lightning to her being attacked by Satanists. However, there had been no storm the night before and there were no tracks – vehicular, human or animal – anywhere near the carcass. The only prints found were the colt's hoof-prints, and these ended about thirty yards from its body. This was a mystery in itself. However, some strange exhaust marks were found on the ground nearby which contained higher than normal levels of radiation. This provided a clue. Many local people had reported seeing strange lights in the sky and Berle Lewis's mother had seen a large craft passing over her cabin, the day Lady disappeared.

The mutilation of Lady was not an isolated case. It was the first of a spate of animal mutilations in Colorado. Later that year, it spread to Pennsylvania. These were followed by a wave of mutilations in Alabama, Iowa and Texas. In the 1970s in the US alone, over ten thousand cattle were discovered with organs surgically removed and corpses drained of blood. Hundreds of mutilations occurred in some areas. Since then cattle have been found dead and mutilated in forty-nine out of the fifty states and reports have come in from around the world.

What's more, strange cases of animal mutilation are not just a recent phenomenon. Accounts of unexplained sheep mutilations in Britain and Australia also occurred in the nineteenth century. The earliest known account that links UFOs to mutilations comes from an edition of the *Farmers' Advocate* published in Yates Center, Kansas, on the 23 April 1897. Local farmer Alexander Hamilton made a sworn statement describing how he had been woken by bawling cows. He looked outside to find 'an airship slowly descending on my cow lot about 40 rods [220 yards] from the house'. It was a cigar-shaped craft around three hundred feet long and it turned a beam of light on him. The ship made a buzzing noise and rose up to about five hundred feet, taking one of his heifers with it. Next day he was told that the head, legs and hide of the cow had been found.

A famous encounter that occurred in May 1973 may hold a clue to why this is happening. It happened when Judy Doraty, Judy's daughter Cindy Doraty, Judy's mother and Judy's sister-in-law were driving near Houston, Texas. The women suddenly saw a strange light hovering in the sky. They stopped the car and got out to take a closer look. Eventually the object disappeared. They then returned to the car and went on their way.

Later Judy began to experience anxiety attacks and severe headaches. Several doctors examined her and drew a blank. Finally she was referred to UFOlogist Dr Leo Sprinkle.

Under hypnosis she described what she had seen: 'It's like a spotlight shining down on the back of my car. And it's like it has substance to it... I'm looking up. I can see an animal being taken up into this... I can see it squirming and trying to get free. And it's like it's being sucked up. It's taken into some sort of chamber and I get nauseated watching how to excise parts. It's done very quickly, but the calf doesn't die immediately. The calf's heart isn't taken... and then I can see the calf being lowered and when it's on the ground I can see it's not moving...'

When asked how the animal was being cut up, she said: 'With instruments... they are like a knife but with different handles... the tissue is laid out flat and smooth and there are needles in it, or probes with tubes connected to them. The same thing is happening with the testicles and eyes.'

And she was not alone: 'I feel the presence of things, but I can't see them… It appears to be two little men… Their hands have long claw nails… very large hypnotic eyes, but they don't blink… I did not see a mouth…they talk, but not with their mouths… they said I wasn't supposed to be here… they project that it was necessary this be done and that it is for the benefit of mankind – and that they are watching us.'

She then went on to mention seeing her daughter Cindy on an 'operating' table.

'They don't listen, they just ignore me,' Judy went on. 'They go about their work as if it's nothing. They don't seem to have any emotions. They don't seem to care. They just take some samples from her.'

Later Cindy was also hypnotised and recalled events which clearly backed up her mother's accounts. She described two 'mantis-like' creatures that moved 'mechanically like robots'. She recounted seeing a calf being raised into a spaceship by a yellow beam.

'It acts like it's bawling,' she said, 'but you can't hear it.'

This case provided the first link between animal mutilations and alien abductions. However, alien abduction was still a relatively poorly understood phenomenon at the time and this connection only fuelled the controversy.

Even so, the subject of animal mutilations could not be lightly dismissed. There was another outbreak in Colorado in the early 1980s and another in the Deep South in the early 1990s. In between, isolated cases have occurred across America with similar reports coming from Puerto Rico, Canada, Mexico, Central and South America, Australia, Russia and parts of Europe.

Mutilation UK

British UFO researcher Tony Dodd has amassed a huge file of animal mutilations that have occurred in the UK. They exhibit the same hallmarks as the US cases: the 'surgical removal' of internal organs along with tongues and eyes; bloodless wounds; jawbones stripped of flesh and rectums cored out. Following a spate of cat mutilations in Texas in 1991, where moggies had been drained of blood and subjected to intense heat, cat killing spread to the UK. In 1999, numerous cats were found decapitated or disembowelled.

Since 1990, Dodd has found that wild animals – deer, badgers, foxes, seals and birds – have been mutilated as well as livestock. There was a particular outbreak in North Yorkshire in 1998, where spinal cords, optic nerves, digestive systems and brains were removed. However, both the Nation Union of Farmers and the National Veterinary College deny all knowledge of mutilations. But Dodd says that individual vets have frequently told him that they have found dead sheep with their organs missing and their bodies drained of blood. British cases also report a small hole bored in the cranium.

And Dodd is convinced that there is a connection between these mutilations and alien intruders.

'There have been reports of dead animals falling from the sky, often coinciding with UFO sightings,' he says.

Alien Sushi

Mutilation cases have also been reported in Japan. On 29 December 1990, a farmer in the Saga Prefecture was woken by the loud and continuous barking of his dog. He went out to see what all

Cow found dead with half its tongue and four teats cut away, 29 December 1990, in Kinryuu Town, Saga Prefecture, Japan.

the fuss was about. When he entered the cow shed, he found a twelve-month-old cow lying on the floor with its tongue missing and the nipples from its udders removed.

Then on 4 January 1993, his dog began barking again. This time he rushed out to the cow shed and was just in time to observe a small white object floating in the air next to a cow. The object quickly moved outside and disappeared. The second cow, however, was more fortunate. It only suffered a broken leg.

Prize Bull

One of the most famous animal mutilation cases of recent times, was discovered on 5 August 1999. It was a bright and sunny morning when cattle rancher Milo Hauck went out to start work on his farm in Menno, South Dakota. He began, like every other day, with a check on the cattle. But when Hauck went to visit his 350-pound prize bull, he was confronted with a sickening sight. The prized animal was lying face down in the mud, its lifeless body strangely mutilated. Its genitals had been removed by a circular, bloodless incision and its rectum had been neatly cored out.

Hauck looked around for some clue to who could have done such a thing. But, even though the ground was muddy, there were no tracks. Even more puzzling was that there was no sign that the fit and aggressive bull had put up a struggle.

Running back to the ranch house, Hauck called the police. When Sheriff Jack Holden arrived, he could offer Hauck little help. Holden was as mystified as Hauck by the bizarre mutilation. But one thing that he did notice was that the barbed wire fence of the bull's pen was underneath the dead animal. For this to have happened, the bull must have fallen on it from above. And judging by how deeply the carcass was embedded in the ground, it must have fallen from quite some height.

Case Studies

Most mutilations involve cattle, although sheep, goats, horses, domestic pets and even wild animals have occasionally been victims. And the vast majority of cases follow a remarkably similar

Retired New Mexico Sandia Labs electronics specialist Howard Burgess. In an experiment, a herd passed through ultraviolet light by Burgess were found to have fluorescent splashes and he believed they may have been marked for airborne identification.

pattern. Usually, there is no trace of a struggle. Even in muddy or snow-covered ground, no tracks or footprints are found near the carcass. However, there are sometimes indications that the animals have somehow been lifted off the ground and dumped where they are found from the air. Generally, the internal organs, eyes, ears, tongues, rectums and genitalia, along with flesh from the jaw, have been surgically removed and are missing. Bloodless incisions – often deep and circular or oval in shape – are also found. Many of the carcasses are completely drained of blood. Again, these incisions are made with surgical precision.

Microscopic analysis of the tissue has shown that some of the cuts are made by a scalpel. But others appear to have been made without a knife. In some cases the incision seems to have been made by cutting between the cells, without tearing them – which would be impossible using any normal technique. Sometimes there are traces of 'cooking', which a pathologist's report said was 'consistent with a heat-induced injury' as if the flesh has been cut with a laser. However, none of the carbon deposits normally left by lasers have been found. Nevertheless, the wound was 'consistent with a specimen collected via electrosurgical excision'. So are the aliens here taking medical samples?

The phenomenon left pathologist investigators unfamiliar with alien abductions baffled. Experienced ranchers and sheriffs who have been called to cattle mutilations for decades are convinced that they could not possibly be the work of indigenous predators, such as mountain lions, wolves or coyotes. They would leave messy wounds when they ate their prey. The clean and precise wounds on the carcasses show that something else is involved. But what? Since the 1970s, cattlemen's associations have posted rewards for information – to no avail.

In exhaustive undercover operations, US and Canadian state authorities investigated the possible involvement of satanic cults. They have failed to find any link between occult activity and these mutilations. And no one could explain what kind of strange diabolical ritual involved the use of bulky medical lasers and helicopters – or what kind of sect would have access to such things.

However, mysterious, low-flying black helicopters were often seen in the area immediately before or after the discovery of a mutilated carcass. They were often silent and carried none of the identification numbers required by Federal regulations. On several occasions, the helicopters were seen spraying the area where mutilated animals were subsequently found. This gave rise to speculation that livestock was being used for testing chemical and biological weapons by covert government agencies.

Government Involvement

Another explanation comes from former police officer turned cattle-mutilation researcher Ted Oliphant, who investigated a spate of mutilations in the small town of Fyffe, Alabama in the 1990s. He believes that the mutilations are part of a massive US government experiment, using helicopters and cutting-edge technology to monitor the spread of infectious diseases, especially Bovine Spongiform Encephalopathy (BSE) or 'mad-cow disease'. Oliphant insists that such apparently clumsy, dangerous and clandestine methods are the only way to monitor the spread of disease across a wide territory.

During his investigations, a large number of unmarked helicopters were spotted in the area where the cattle had been mutilated. One case that linked the helicopters to the mutilations occurred in February 1993, when farmer Keith Davis was woken by a helicopter. In the morning, he found that his cattle had been horridly mutilated. Oliphant submitted the victims' tissue for laboratory analysis. This found a cocktail of human pharmaceuticals, including synthetic amphetamines, anti-coagulants, barbiturates and other chemicals that had no place in a cow. 'Military personnel in helicopters are doing one of three things,' says Oliphant. 'They may be conducting the mutilations themselves. They may be using helicopters to investigate the mutilations once they have been carried out by another, possibly extraterrestrial, source. Finally, they may be tampering with existing mutilations to imply that the military was responsible.'

US military and intelligence agencies have consistently denied any involvement in animal mutilations. And the Federal Aviation Authority has denied the very existence of these strange helicopters. Witnesses who have photographed these helicopters have found themselves threatened by men wearing black uniforms without insignia.

Although the official explanation for animal mutilations has always been natural causes, the FBI bowed to public pressure in 1979 and began investigating the phenomenon. Its 279-page report was published the following year. Again natural causes were cited as the culprit. The cause of death could be linked to parasites, the report said. Official government autopsies cited showed that the lack of blood was consistent with the length of time the dead animals had been left undisturbed. It largely sided with those who believed that the mutilations were the work of animal predators. Outraged ranchers complained that the report was a whitewash. They formed vigilante groups and shot at any low-flying helicopters crossing their fields.

Strange Harvest

Award-winning documentary film-maker Linda Moulton Howe began investigating the phenomenon. She had already won Emmies for her documentaries on medical, environmental and scientific subjects when, in October 1975, she got a call from her brother who was a helicopter pilot stationed at the ICBM silo at Malmstrom, Montana. He had seen an 'orange glowing disc the size of a football field' hovering over the silo. It cast a 'light brighter than daylight'. The following day, it was discovered that the missiles' targeting systems had been scrambled and eventually, the missiles had to be replaced. What initially sparked Linda Howe's interest was the fact that several ranchers discovered mutilated animals in the same area. The veterinary surgeon who examined the carcasses reported that he had seen a cow with its lips removed in precise 'bevelled' cuts. The animal's blood had been

Cattle mutilation at Morrill Farm, Piermont, New Hampshire, 27 September 1978.

drained from its body so completely that the tissue was left a pinkish white.

She produced her first documentary on animal mutilations, *A Strange Harvest*, in 1980. Since then she has become an authority on the subject. In 1989, she wrote *An Alien Harvest*, following its success with *Glimpses of Other Realities* in 1993.

In 1993, in some cases in Alabama, she showed that even the mutilated animals' capillaries – as well as their arteries and veins – had been drained of blood. This could not have occurred had the livestock been attacked by predators. Besides, what predators would be so particular as only to take the genitalia and other specific organs? Carnivores, humans included, go for the meat – that is, the muscle; the very thing the mutilators leave behind.

She believes that this points to the fact that the mystery assailants are extraterrestrial in origin. Since her 1980 documentary *A Strange Harvest* first brought the cattle mutilation phenomenon to international attention she has amassed a huge body of evidence which, she claims, points strongly towards alien intervention.

Like other investigators, in the course of her research, she has noted that mutilations always conform to a repeated set of characteristics.

New Mexico State Police Officer Gabe Valdez, who in the 1970s coordinated vigorous interstate investigations of livestock mutilations, examining a mutilated carcass in Rio Arriba county.

'An eye and an ear are often missing,' she says. 'Flesh from the jaw is stripped off on one side only, bones are cut cleanly without a trace of bone chippings, indicating a saw was not used. The tongue is always severed with a vertical cut deep in the throat... The animal's rectum is always cored out, and various internal organs are removed. The cuts are usually bloodless.'

In many cases Howe investigated the bodies of the animals have been completely drained of blood. This is often done via a small hole punched in the jugular vein. The evidence indicates that the animals are still alive when this is done. This has led Howe to speculate that advanced technology is being used in this procedure. She cites one case, which occurred in Arkansas, in March 1989, where five pregnant cows were mutilated and an unborn calf was removed through an incision while still in its embryonic sac. Under forensic examination it was shown that the fluid inside the sac had evaporated completely. This indicated the presence of a searing heat. This theory gets some corroboration from the work of Dr John Altshuler, who has undertaken a number of private investigations since being involved in the Lady case. His microscopic examination of tissues taken from the incised areas of mutilated animals has shown that some had been exposed to temperatures of over 350°C. Even more mysteriously, it was found that the cells surrounding the incision were individually parted and not damaged or split, as would occur if a knife had been used. To Howe and others, this indicates that the cutting is done using highly sophisticated technology, possibly a laser-like instrument not of terrestrial origin.

FBI Involvement

Although the FBI had officially stated that animal mutilations could be put down to natural causes, they had good reason to believe otherwise. UFO author Timothy Good obtained a secret 1976 FBI report which contains the testimony of Officer Gabriel Valdez of the New Mexico State Police. After being called to an animal mutilation, Valdez discovered a series of strange depressions in the earth. Each indentation had a diameter of sixteen inches and the marks formed a series of equilateral triangles. To Valdez, this strongly suggested that a 'suspected aircraft' had landed, then taken off again, followed the cow and landed again where the cow was

A mutilated carcass found in northern New Mexico, USA, in the 1970s.

killed. An oily yellow substance was found at the landing sites. The grass there was scorched and radiation level at those sites was much higher than the surrounding area.

When this report saw the light of day, it confirmed what UFOlogists had long suspected. State investigators and ranchers became convinced too. The chief investigator of mutilations for the District Attorney's office in Trinidad, Colorado, Lou Girodo, said plainly: 'We were dealing with creatures not from this planet.'

The UFO Connection

Lady's mutilation, in September 1967, had coincided with a wave of UFO sightings and reports of strange lights in the San Luis Valley. Each subsequent outbreak was heralded by a new wave of UFO sightings. Some UFOlogists speculate that there is a connection between the UFO sightings and the helicopters. A few believed that the UFOs disguise themselves as helicopters.

It is not surprising that animal mutilations occur at the UFO hotspot Dulce, New Mexico. A curious feature of the mutilations there was the presence of fluorescent paint – visible only under ultraviolet light – on the hides of some of the victims. In another case, a putty-like material was found in a cow's ribcage. Analysis showed that substance was chemically related to paint – though researchers are still puzzled about how it got inside the animal.

In her 1989 documentary, *Alien Life Forms,* Linda Moulton Howe interviewed farmers who had witnessed extraterrestrials engaged in the abduction of animals. But she was warned off this line of investigation.

'That documentary you did about cattle mutilations upset some people in Washington. They don't want mutilations and UFOs connected together,' USAF special agent Richard Doty told her.

No doubt the authorities in Washington were doubly upset when they heard from the numerous eyewitnesses whose accounts made a direct link between UFOs and cattle mutilations. One such came from Dwain Wright, a UCLA graduate, who found a cow suspended in the branches of a tree in Sands Springs, Oregon, in 1979. A year later, Wright was in the vicinity again and met a cowboy who told him of a wave of UFO sightings in the area. The cowboy then showed Wright a dead bull that was half-buried in mud as if it had been dropped from a great height. The animal had been mutilated and its genitals removed. The cowboy later told Wright how he had seen cattle being floated off the ground and into glowing discs in the sky.

A more spectacular incident was witnessed by Timothy Flint, a medical assistant from Portland, Oregon. On the evening of 29 August 1987, Flint had retired for the night and was about to go to bed when he, quite inexplicably, found himself standing in a field in the dark. Then he saw a strange craft. It sent a beam of light down, which levitated a cow.

'The cow was still eating,' said Flint. 'It don't know this dome-shaped thing was there. All of a sudden this light beam came down from a blue base of a round lighted object in the sky... It came down, surrounded the cow and started to levitate it.'

Flint described how the cow was taken up to the top of the beam where it came into contact with something that emitted a sound like a power saw. The animal was mutilated while floating high in the sky and then dropped earthward.

Then in July 1993, Ron and Paula Watson were standing on the porch of their ranch in Mount Vernon, Missouri, when they saw something strange happening at the far end of their pasture. With a pair of binoculars, they saw a cow lying on its side. It looked like it was paralysed. Two small creatures with large white heads, dressed in silver suits, were standing over the stricken animal. They waved their arms over the cow and it began to float. They raised it until it was over six feet off the ground, then steered it up a ramp into their cone-shaped spaceship. The Watsons had not spotted the ship before because its mirrored surface reflected the surrounding foliage, making it practically invisible. Once the carcass was on board, the aliens followed it up the ramp. The ramp was then retracted, and the ship took off, and vanished into the sky at incredible speed.

The question remains, if the mystery assailants are indeed extra-terrestrial in origin, what is the reason for their interventions?

Alien Abductions

Many UFO researchers believe that the key to this question lies in the connection between animal mutilations and alien abductions. Indeed, it has been suggested that both cattle mutilations and abductions are being conducted by the same extraterrestrial group, and for similar reasons.

Dr John Mack, Professor of Psychiatry at Harvard Medical School, is a researcher who has performed long-standing work with abductees. He says those who have direct contact with aliens are told at least part of the agenda behind their abductions and the related phenomenon of animal mutilations. From abductees' accounts, Mack has discovered that humankind's environmental destruction of the Earth has stimulated the intervention of various groups of alien intelligences. Both mutilations and abductions are a wake-up call to humankind, warning of an impending environmental crisis, he says.

Mack also believes that some alien groups have a problem with reproduction and they have carried out abductions and mutilations as a means of extracting human and animal DNA. Their aim is to fuse it with their own in order to advance their evolution.

His view is supported Linda Howe. In her book *Glimpses of Other Realities,* she recounts the case of Jeanne Robinson, who is in telepathic communication with an alien intelligence. During one exchange, the extraterrestrial explained why they were performing the mutilations.

'We use substances from cows in an essential biochemical process for our survival,' it said. 'The material we use from cattle contains the correct amount of protein needed for biochemical absorption… While we respect all life, some sacrifices are made for the preservation of other species.'

Another link between alien abductions and animal mutilations is the presence of 'Greys' – small aliens with bulbous heads, big black almond-shaped eyes and claw-like hands. Linda Howe has information from various 'confidential sources' – including people in the military and intelligence agencies – confirming the involvement of Greys in animal mutilations. 'One of these Grey groups has some kind of survival problem,' she has been told, 'and at least one of the reasons for animal mutilations is to gather enough fluid, I guess from haemoglobin and the plasma, to make some kind of essential bio-chemical ingredient that these creatures need.'

But why would a technologically advanced species, capable of travelling billions of miles across space to visit Earth, need our livestock to cure their medical problems?

Goat-Suckers

Greys are not the only species of aliens who mutilate animals. In Caribbean countries and Latin America, witnesses have seen a strange breed of extraterrestrial lizard, which is thought to be responsible for the attacks. The mutilated animals are usually found with a number of small holes bored into the neck or head. In many cases, all the blood has been drained from the body. For this reason, the local population has named this strange creature *El Chupacabra,* or the 'Goat-sucker'.

Sightings began in early 1995 on the Caribbean island of Puerto Rico. One of the first reliable eyewitness reports was made by a police officer who went to investigate the mutilation of a sheep. While he was inspecting the carcass, he became aware that something was observing him from the shadows. When he turned around, he saw a strange creature. It was about five feet tall, with dark skin and orange-yellow eyes. As it made off, he tried to pursue it, but he quickly developed a throbbing headache, was overcome with nausea and collapsed.

A more detailed description was provided by Luis Guadaloupe, a resident of the town of Canovanas. In October 1995, he walked into the police station there and reported his encounter with a bizarre creature, which he had seen flying through the air while he was out walking.

'It was really ugly, like a demon,' Guadaloupe said. 'It was around four to five feet tall, with huge, elongated eyes. It moved like a kangaroo by jumping from powerful back legs. It had a long pointed tongue, which moved in and out of its mouth.'

Its skin was mainly grey, but its back seemed to change colour, and it gave off a foul sulphurous stench.

Normally, such a story would have been dismissed by the police. But they took Guadaloupe's sighting seriously because there were so many similar sightings already on file. Some people had reported that there was a series of spines, about ten inches long, down the creature's back. These, it seemed, were responsible for the colour change. They also made a buzzing sound. Other witnesses said it smelled like animal urine or battery acid, rather than sulphur – but anyway, nothing pleasant.

Since 1995, there have been numerous other sightings of this creature. It has been linked to the grisly slaughter and mutilation of animals. By 1997, well over 2,500 had fallen victim. Throughout the island, farmers have lost all sorts of livestock, including cattle, sheep and goats, as well as cats, dogs, rabbits, rats and birds. Examination of their mutilated bodies shows that the blood has been sucked from them through small holes bored in the head and neck – hence the local name for creature, 'Chupacabra', or goatsucker. The incisions are clean, as if made by a surgical instrument. The owner of some livestock killed in Puerto Rico on 12 August 1998 said: 'The animals were sucked dry and appeared as if cut by a double-edged surgical knife.'

The teeth or claws of a predator would leave a ragged wound and signs of a struggle. Vets also point out that if a wild animal grabs another creature by the neck, its teeth cause wounding to both sides of the neck. This does not occur to victims of Chupacabras.

Other bizarre findings include strange triangular wounds in the liver of a sheep that had been drained of blood and mutilated sheep on the farm of Radames Marin in Yuco; Puerto Rico, that showed no signs of rigor mortis.

ABEs and UFOs

Jorge Martin, editor of the magazine *Evidencia OVNI* and Puerto Rico's leading investigator into the Chupacabras phenomenon, prefers to call the creatures Anomalous Biological Entities (ABEs).

He believes there is a link between ABEs and UFO activity, as UFOs are often seen hovering over the area where the mutilated remains of animals are found. Reports from investigators and eye-witnesses suggest that ABEs or Chupacabras are unlike any known species. This has led a number of researchers to conclude that they are of extraterrestrial origin. Another faction say that the Chupacabras are the product of some hideous covert genetic experiment conducted by the US military. The allegation is that the military is using the off-shore island as an experimental 'playground' for testing illegal weapons. In the past, a variety of top-secret pro jects, involving everything from Thalidomide and Agent Orange to radiation weapons, were based on the island. These practices have gone on for years.

In 1932, the Rockefeller Institute's chief pathologist said: 'The Puerto Ricans are the dirtiest, laziest, most degenerate and thievish race of men ever inhabiting this sphere... all physicians take delight in the abuse and torture of these unfortunate subjects.'

Many people on the island have been given cancer or infected with fatal diseases to further US research. As late as the 1980s, male prison inmates on Puerto Rico were being injected with female hormones as part of an experiment.

'At first I believed these animals were the result of some genetic or bionic experiment, but I now believe that they are not terrestrial in origin,' says Martin. 'Over twenty per cent of people who see this strange creature also report witnessing some sort of aerial phenomena. These witnesses – separated socially as well as geographically – give remarkably similar UFO descriptions. I don't think this can be ignored when trying to understand the Chupacabra problem.'

Puerto Rico has been a centre for UFO activity for many years. Many Chupacabra witnesses report seeing luminous pyramid-shaped craft, and reports of animal mutilations invariably increase the day after these sightings.

Martin published an artist's impression of a Chupacabra, based on a number of eyewitness descriptions, and widely considered to be the most accurate. It shows a lizard-like creature, although it has a stockier body and longer legs. Significantly, it has large, dark, almond-shaped eyes.

Hundreds of people all over Puerto Rico have seen similar creatures, though there are significant differences in the descriptions they give. This has led researchers to believe that there may be a number of different species on the island. Some are hairy; others have scaly skin. Some, like the one Guadaloupe saw, can fly. Another witness saw a creature with vestigial wings, perched in trees. It then launched itself from the branches and glided down on to its prey.

'We are telling people to keep the women and children locked up inside at night,' one villager told the local TV station. 'No one really knows what it is.'

Martin spoke for many of the local population when he expressed his anger at the lack of official action. Whether the creatures were terrestrial or alien, valuable livestock was being slaughtered.

'Right now, I would say the situation is out of control,' Martin said in 1996. 'It's happening everywhere, and government officials who are elected by us to solve our problems are not doing this at the moment.'

Official Reaction

The authorities tried to dismiss the sightings as hysteria and blamed the mutilations on human mischief. However, public pressure forced them to arrange for government veterinarians to conduct an official autopsy of twenty mutilated animals in front of an audience of invited journalists to establish the facts.

After this public examination of the mutilated animals, the head of the government's Agricultural Department of Veterinarian Services Dr Hector Garcia was still prepared to dismiss the possibility of attack by Chupacabras as the cause of death.

'The autopsy revealed a variety of causes of death, including parasites,' he announced. 'I believe the attacks are most likely due to feral dogs or a rhesus monkey imported to Puerto Rico for scientific experiments.'

And Angel Luis, a veterinarian at the island's Gardenville Clinic, said: 'It could be a human being who belongs to a religious sect, even another animal. It could also be someone who wants to make fun out of the Puerto Rican people.'

These statements were greeted with ridicule, and investigators accused the government of conducting a cover-up. They point out that the official explanations, such as attacks by predators or hoaxers, make little sense when you take into account the huge number of animals being killed. The authorities made no attempt to explain the strange mutilations and the physical evidence on the victims. Nor did they take into account the numerous eyewitness accounts.

Jorge Martin accuses the authorities of ignoring the evidence rather than admitting their ignorance. But he says that something may be going on behind the scenes.

'I have confidential sources that have informed me that two Chupacabras have been captured by the authorities here, and are being studied in conjunction with US investigators,' he says. 'So, while animals are dying and the farmers are panicking about their livelihood, there is a possibility that someone, somewhere, knows exactly what is going on.'

To Catch a Chupacabra

The noted UFO researcher Professor G. C. Schellhorn has investigated a number of reports from people who have tried to kill or capture Chupacabras. In one case, Canovanas policeman Juan Collazo shot at one at point-blank range. He hit the creature – to no apparent effect. A fire chief managed to scare a Chupacabra away by shooting at it. Afterwards, he discovered what he believed to be Chupacabra hair caught on a barbed wire fence.

Another case occurred in the town of Gurabo, when a man named Jesus Sanchez found the bodies of his rabbits dead in his backyard. Suspecting that a Chupacabra might be responsible, he mounted a vigil and wait for the creature to return. A few days later, when the Chupacabra came back at 4 a.m., Sanchez was ready. He dazzled it with a powerful torch and tried to kill it with two blows of his machete.

'It sounded like I had struck a hollow drum,' he told Schellhorn. Apparently unharmed, the creature escaped.

The situation in Canovanas became so serious that, despite official opposition, the town's mayor, former police detective Jose Soto, got involved. After examining the evidence of mutilation, he had no choice but to take people's fear of the Chupacabra seriously. He organised a number of expeditions to try to capture a Chupacabra. With the help of the local civil defence unit, he assembled two hundred heavily-armed volunteers and laid traps around the jungles of El Yunque in the Cubuy region of Puerto Rico, an area which has long been a hot spot for paranormal and UFO sightings. So far they have come up empty-handed.

Soto is furious that his pleas to the island's governor and the police chief have largely been ignored.

'Whatever it is,' he said, 'it's highly intelligent. Today it's attacking animals, but tomorrow it may attack people.'

Soto feels that he has no choice but to take the matter into his own hands.

'I am engaged in a search for this creature,' he said. 'If I can capture one of them I will make it public at once. I won't allow anyone to come and take it away.'

In the mean time, Puerto Ricans are exploiting the situation for all it is worth. They have developed quite a Chupacabra industry – along the lines of the Scottish exploitation of the Loch Ness Monster. You can buy posters, key rings, tee-shirts and golf bags, all with the image of a Chupacabra on it.

'This is not a joking matter,' says Martin. 'Whatever is killing these farm animals is seriously affecting the economy. Some people may laugh at the Chupacabras, but people here stay inside at night and lock their doors.'

Sightings Spread

Although Chupacabra sightings began around the town of Canovanas, they spread to forty of Puerto Rico's seventy municipalities within four months. In 1997, a spate of new attacks were reported from the town of Utuado, forty miles south-west of the capital San Juan. Some forty-two rabbits, a number of chickens and a duck were found dead on farm on 20 November. All of the animals had twin, triangular perforations on their bodies, mostly in the region of the stomach. Researcher Scott Corrales was called in.

'One rabbit had its stomach split by an incision so precise it could only have been made by a surgical instrument used by an expert surgeon,' he said. 'No trace of blood remained in any of the dead animals.'

On 12 August 1998, residents of Barrio Playa near San Juan found a number of dead animals in their back yards. Police officer Rogelio Orsini reported that a total of seventeen rabbits, four guinea hens, two hens, four chicks and one rooster were found dead – 'victims of a strange Chupacabra-like assailant'. According to his report: 'The animals presented perforations on their necks or stomachs and were completely bloodless.'

A trained criminal investigator, Officer Orsini concluded: 'This is not the handiwork of a dog or an ordinary animal, given the number of animals killed and the strangeness of the circumstances. The animals have two perforations made with some kind of sharp object and have no blood in them. This is strange, very strange.'

Reports were soon coming from all areas of the island, which has led Professor Schellhorn to conclude that the creature is very mobile or is breeding extremely rapidly.

Mexican Mutilations

Chupacabra attacks are now no longer an exclusively Puerto Rican problem. They are now being seen in Florida, Texas, California and, particularly, Mexico. On 19 August 1998, Chupacabras struck at a small farm on the outskirts of Monterrey. A peasant farmer, so scared by the attack that he would be identified only by the name 'Rodrigo', reported that two of his chickens had died mysteriously. Examining one of the bodies, he was shocked to find that its internal organs were gone and its blood had been removed.

Mexican TV journalist and UFOlogist Jaime Maussan turned his attention to Chupacabra sightings.

'There have been hundreds of attacks in Mexico,' Maussan says.

'In some cases more than sixty animals were killed. All of them have been found with circular holes, usually in the neck. I don't know if it's of ET origin or a genetic experiment, all I know is it's real.'

In Puerto Rico, Chupacabras activity has been limited to animal mutilation, but Maussan has investigated several cases in Mexico where people have been attacked. He has interviewed people who shake with terror and begin to sob. Maussan is in no doubt that they are telling the truth. 'Believe me, it's a very scary experience,' he says.

In Puerto Rico too, Chupacabras are sometimes threatening. On 9 November 1995, Ada Arroyo, the assistant director of the Mount Sion Nursing Home near Barrio Turabo Arriba in Caguas, had a nervous breakdown after seeing a Chupacabra. At around 7 p.m., Senora Arroyo heard screams 'like those made by a lamb being slaughtered'. When she went outside to investigate, she saw a 'strange hairy figure, greyish in colour, covering its body with a pair of wings'. It had 'a flattened, vulpine face with enormous red eyes'. The creature held her gaze with its hypnotic eyes before spreading its wings and soaring into the air.

It is unclear how the Chupacabras got from Puerto Rico to the mainland. The island are separated from Florida by over a thousand miles of water, but there are reports there of bizarre creatures that match the descriptions of the Chupacabras seen in Puerto Rico. They have spread across the south and are now emerging in California.

In 1998, British cryptozoologist Jonathan Downes and colleague Graham Inglis travelled though Mexico, Puerto Rico and Florida in search of Chupacabras. Their first stop was the state of Puebla in Central Mexico. There, with local vet Soledad de la Pena, they went to visit the smallholding of a farmer named Dom Pedro. In July 1996, Soledad had been called to Dom Pedro's farm after he had found three of his sheep mysteriously mutilated. Downes and Inglis found the walls of many of Dom Pedro's village daubed with crosses. This, Dom Pedro explained, was *'por protectione de vampiros'*. In Mexico, people call Chupacabras *'vampiros'*. Despite the crosses, the church has refused to get involved.

Dom Pedro's case was of particular interest to Downes because, unusually, at least one of the three sheep in question had remained alive for some time after the attack. Soledad had arrived at Dom Pedro's some twelve hours after the attack and had videoed her examination of the victims. The video shows Soledad putting her gloved hand through an enormous hole in the chest of one of the sheep and into the thoracic cavity itself. But when she withdrew her hand, the glove had no more than tiny traces of blood upon it. According to Soledad, the animal been completely drained of its blood.

Although there were two massive holes in the animal's body – one drilled completely through the bones of the rib cage – and some of its internal organs were missing, somehow the animal was still alive. Soledad had no medical explanation for this.

Downes and Inglis then travelled to the village of Tlaloxitcan, about a hundred miles to the south, to investigate another series of reported attacks. These had taken place on the same night as the mutilation of Dom Pedro's sheep. An elderly farmhand named Juan volunteered a description of the attacks. That night, ten households in the village had been attacked simultaneously. Early in the evening they had seen strange lights in the sky. Then, at about midnight, people from the ten households were woken up by the pitiful cries of their goats and sheep. The animals were being attacked by an unknown predator. In all, thirty animals – three from each household – had been mutilated. All of them had been completely drained of blood. Here, though, the blood of the victims splashed across the ground, which is unusual in Chupacabra attacks. There was another key difference. This was an Indian village – Dom Pedro's village was peopled by descendants of the Spaniards.

In Downes' book *Only Fools and Goat-suckers – the Search for the Chupacabra,* he hypothesises that the phenomenon somehow mirrors the religious background of the local people. Where there are Catholics, who believe that blood of Christ is consumed during Holy Communion, the blood of the Chupacabra's victims is also consumed, whereas in Tlaloxitcan, which is inhabited by the descendants of Aztecs who gloried in the ritual spilling of blood, the Chupacabra follow suit. Downes does not know why this should be, but it clearly indicates that there is an intelligent force behind the Chupacabra attacks.

From Downes' research it is clear that there was a connection between Chupacabra attacks and UFO activity. However, he was unable to pin down the precise nature of the Chupacabra itself.

'Confusing the issue is the wide variety of eyewitness reports,' Downes says, 'many of which describe creatures with vastly differing morphologies, and all of which have, at one time or another, been identified as the "true" Chupacabra. The creatures described have ranged from ape-like animals and bizarre winged creatures, to flying cat-like animals and archetypal bipedal, kangaroo-like creatures with a row of spines along their backs.'

However, an intriguing photograph has come to light. It originally appeared in the 25 September 1996 issue of the *De Quincy News*, in De Quincy, Louisiana, under the headline 'What is it?' The picture had been taken by a woman named Barbara Mullins and showed a strange-looking creature covered with thick woolly hair, which she had found dead at the roadside. The creature was the size of a very large dog, Mullins said. The animal also had the general appearance of a dog, except for the face, which looked like a baboon's. In October 1998, veteran investigator Loren Coleman show the picture to students at a US veterinary school. They concluded that the animal was, indeed, a dog.

'The canine has manicured toenails, not claws, is petite footed, not webbed, as perhaps would be found on an expensive show quality dog,' they said. 'It looks as if it was also recently groomed as the muzzle and paws have been shaved in typical poodle and Pomeranian styles.'

This was a case of mistaken identity. But it will come as no comfort to the farmers in Mexico and Puerto Rico who continue to lose their livestock, and their livelihood, on an almost nightly basis.

More disturbing is the strange connection that has been made between the flying Chupacabras that have been seen and the phenomenon of airborne 'rods'. Recently a number of Mexican newspapers have reported that a strange airborne creature resembling 'a flying manta ray' was videotaped by Jose Eriverto Lopez de la Garza over Monterrey, where Santiago Ytturia first filmed rods. According to the reports, the creature 'can be seen in a number of slow-motion frames of the video recording'. Again, this was how rods were first identified. The creature's skin is greenish and it has a membrane that connects its arms to its thorax – something commonly reported by those who see Chupacabras.

4 Conspiracies of Silence

All the President's Men

In December 1984, the mailman delivered a package to Hollywood movie producer and UFOlogist Jaime Shandera. Inside there was a roll of undeveloped black and white 35mm film. There was no letter accompanying it. The package carried no return address, though the postmark said Albuquerque, New Mexico.

Shandera had the film processed. It showed an eight-page government document dated 18 November 1952 and a briefing paper for the then president-elect Dwight Eisenhower, who would be sworn in the following January. The first page said: 'This is a TOP SECRET – EYES ONLY document containing compartmentalised information essential to the national security of the United States.'

Page two listed the twelve top US intelligence experts, military leaders and scientists involved in its preparation. Then, on page three, what the paper was about was revealed. It said explicitly that in July 1947, a 'flying disc-shaped aircraft' had crashed near Roswell, New Mexico, and 'extra-terrestrial biological entities' had been recovered by the military.

Attached to the briefing paper was a copy of a memorandum, dated 24 September 1947. It was from President Eisenhower's predecessor, Harry S. Truman, to James Forrestal, the Secretary of Defense in the Truman administration. In it, Truman instructs Forrestal to proceed with 'Operation Majestic-12'. Read in conjunction with the briefing paper, it became clear that Majestic-12 was a twelve-man committee set up by Defense Secretary Forrestal to handle the possibility of an alien invasion at Roswell. Its members were the high-flyers listed on page two. The briefing paper also made the national security implications clear. The final paragraph stressed the need to 'avoid a public panic at all costs'. This,

TOP SECRET / MAJIC

EYES ONLY

* TOP SECRET *
....

EYES ONLY   COPY ONE OF ONE.

SUBJECT: OPERATION MAJESTIC-12 PRELIMINARY BRIEFING FOR
PRESIDENT-ELECT EISENHOWER.

DOCUMENT PREPARED 18 NOVEMBER, 1952.

BRIEFING OFFICER: ADM. ROSCOE H. HILLENKOETTER (MJ-1)

NOTE: This document has been prepared as a preliminary briefing
only. It should be regarded as introductory to a full operations
briefing intended to follow.

* * * * * *

OPERATION MAJESTIC-12 is a TOP SECRET Research and Development/
Intelligence operation responsible directly and only to the
President of the United States. Operations of the project are
carried out under control of the Majestic-12 (Majic-12) Group
which was established by special classified executive order of
President Truman on 24 September, 1947, upon recommendation by
Dr. Vannevar Bush and Secretary James Forrestal. (See Attachment
"A".) Members of the Majestic-12 Group were designated as follows:

> Adm. Roscoe H. Hillenkoetter
> Dr. Vannevar Bush
> Secy. James V. Forrestal*
> Gen. Nathan F. Twining
> Gen. Hoyt S. Vandenberg
> Dr. Detlev Bronk
> Dr. Jerome Hunsaker
> Mr. Sidney W. Souers
> Mr. Gordon Gray
> Dr. Donald Menzel
> Gen. Robert M. Montague
> Dr. Lloyd V. Berkner

The death of Secretary Forrestal on 22 May, 1949, created
a vacancy which remained unfilled until 01 August, 1950, upon
which date Gen. Walter B. Smith was designated as permanent
replacement.

On 24 June, 1947, a civilian pilot flying over the Cascade
Mountains in the State of Washington observed nine flying
disc-shaped aircraft traveling in formation at a high rate
of speed. Although this was not the first known sighting
of such objects, it was the first to gain widespread attention
in the public media. Hundreds of reports of sightings of
similar objects followed. Many of these came from highly
credible military and civilian sources. These reports res-
ulted in independent efforts by several different elements
of the military to ascertain the nature and purpose of these
objects in the interests of national defense. A number of
witnesses were interviewed and there were several unsuccessful
attempts to utilize aircraft in efforts to pursue reported
discs in flight. Public reaction bordered on near hysteria
at times.

In spite of these efforts, little of substance was learned
about the objects until a local rancher reported that one
had crashed in a remote region of New Mexico located approx-
imately seventy-five miles northwest of Roswell Army Air
Base (now Walker Field).

On 07 July, 1947, a secret operation was begun to assure
recovery of the wreckage of this object for scientific study.
During the course of this operation, aerial reconnaissance
discovered that four small human-like beings had apparently
ejected from the craft at some point before it exploded.
These had fallen to earth about two miles east of the wreckage
site. All four were dead and badly decomposed due to action
by predators and exposure to the elements during the approx-
imately one week time period which had elapsed before their
discovery. A special scientific team took charge of removing
these bodies for study. (See Attachment "C".) The wreckage
of the craft was also removed to several different locations.
(See Attachment "B".) Civilian and military witnesses in
the area were debriefed, and news reporters were given the
effective cover story that the object had been a misguided
weather research balloon.

....
* TOP SECRET *
....

EYES ONLY TOP SECRET / MAJIC   T52-EXEMPT (E)
EYES ONLY

003

the UFO lobby say, is where the government cover-up started.

Leading UFO sceptic Philip Klass, along with researchers Armen Victorian and Kevin Randle, dismissed the documents as clever fakes. But Jaime Shandera and fellow UFOlogist Stanton T. Friedman, who has dedicated over ten years to investigating Roswell, believe they are genuine. They believe that the Majestic-12 papers had been sent to Shandera by one of the many military contacts he had made while researching a 1980 UFO movie.

Other evidence of the activities of Majestic-12 has been pushed through the letter boxes of researchers over the years. A postcard from New Zealand delivered to Bill Moore in 1985 suggested that he take a look through some files at the US National Archives that had recently been declassified. When Moore and Shandera did so, they found a memo confirming the existence of Majestic-12 (also known as MJ-12, or MAJIC). It was addressed to the US Air Force Chief of Staff Nathan Twining and had been written by Robert Cutler, Special Assistant for National Security in the Eisenhower administration.

Between 1992 and 1996, other documents referring to Majestic-12 dropped onto the doormat of Tim Cooper. He sent copies to Friedman. Although several proved to be hoaxes, Cooper and Friedman believe two single-page documents are genuine. One was a memo to President Truman, dictated by US Secretary of State George C. Marshall to his Executive Secretary, R. H. Humelsine. There is no direct mention of MJ-12 in the memo, but the reference code reads: 'MAJIC EO 092447 MJ-12'.

The other was a brief instruction to General Nathan Twining – an MJ-12 member according to the 1952 briefing paper. It concerned his activities during a July 1947 trip to the saucer's crash site in New Mexico.

In 1994, an anonymous informer sent science writer and long-time UFO investigator Don Berliner a roll of film through the post. It carried photographs of twenty-three pages of a 'Majestic-12 Group Special Operations Manual', dated April 1954. The instruction manual was entitled: 'Extra-terrestrial Entities and Technology, Recovery and Disposal.'

Sceptics point out that, as these MJ-12 documents were supplied on film, their veracity cannot be checked by analysing the ink and paper. However, when investigators have found MJ-12 documents in the files, they were printed on onionskin paper of a type supplied in bulk to the US government between 1953 and 1970. There are also numerous factual details that can be checked out. So investigators set about checking out the background of the twelve committee members and the dates of their meetings. They compared the style and format of the MJ-12 documents to other government correspondence and authenticated the signatures.

The Majestic Twelve

The membership of MJ-12 comprised the cream of the military, scientific and intelligence communities. Along with Secretary of Defense Forrestal, there were the secretary of the Army, three generals – two army, one air force – the first three Directors of the Central Intelligence Agency and five of America's top scientists. If you had to pick a top-secret government committee to investigate a UFO crash, this would be it. The members were:

- James V. Forrestal, the first US Secretary of Defense to sit on the cabinet. During World War II he had been in charge of navy procurements. In 1949, he resigned and was hospitalised suffering from depression. Soon after, he committed suicide by throwing himself from his hospital window.
- Gordon Gray, Assistant Secretary of the Army. He became National Security Advisor and Director of the CIA's Psychological Strategy Board.
- General Hoyt Vandenberg, Chief of Military Intelligence during World War II and Director of Central Intelligence from 1946 to 1947.
- Major General Robert Montague, head of the Special Weapons Project at the Atomic Energy Commission at Albuquerque, New Mexico.
- General Nathan F. Twining, Commander of Air Materiel Command at Wright Field. During World War II, he played a

large part in directing the war against the Japanese. In 1957, he was appointed Chairman of the Joint Chiefs of Staff.

• Rear Admiral Roscoe Hillenkoetter, Director of Central Intelligence from 1947 to 1950. In 1960, he acknowledged that there was a UFO cover-up.

• Rear Admiral Sidney Souers, the first Director of Central Intelligence in 1946.

• Dr Vannevar Bush, who was President Truman's scientific advisor and Chairman of the Joint Research and Development Board from 1945 to 1947. During World War II he had been a key player in the development of the atomic bomb.

• Dr Detlev Bronk, a biophysicist who was head of the National Academy of Science and the Chairman of the Medical Advisory Board of the Atomic Energy Committee.

• Dr Lloyd Berkener, Executive Secretary of the Joint Research and Development Board. He became a member of the CIA-funded UFO committee in the 1950s.

• Dr Jerome Hunsaker, Chairman of the National Advisory Committee on Aeronautics and famous aircraft designer.

• Dr Donald Menzel, professor of astrophysics at Harvard and science writer.

But one thing bothered the investigators. All the MJ-12 members had top-level security clearance with the exception of Donald Menzel. He was a well-known UFO sceptic who had written numerous papers debunking flying saucers and three anti-UFO books. However, in April 1986, Stanton Friedman got permission from Menzel's widow and university officials to go through Menzel's papers in the archives at Harvard. In them, he discovered that Menzel had 'Top Secret Ultra' clearance from the CIA and had a thirty-year association with the National Security Agency. He advised the government on numerous classified projects, did highly classified consulting work for many major US corporations and had close connections with the other scientists who sat on MJ-12. He was not just any old astronomy professor and UFO sceptic. In security terms, he was of equal calibre to the rest of the committee.

What's more, Menzel made a number of trips to New Mexico during 1947 and 1948, at government expense.

The other alleged members of the group also checked out. All had worked on top-secret projects and were members of various government research and development boards.

Silent Witnesses

The last member of the committee died just three months before Jaime Shandera received the film, so none of them could be questioned. However, their comings and goings could be traced from telephone logs, minutes from meetings, correspondence and other papers which by that time were on open access in the Library of Congress and various presidential libraries.

The earliest documented reference to Majestic is in the 24 September 1947 memo sent by Truman to Secretary of Defense Forrestal. The memo mentions the president's science advisor Vannevar Bush. Records show that Truman had a meeting with Bush on 24 September – it was the only day between May and December that year they met. Bush also had a meeting with Forrestal on that day.

That same day, a secret memo was sent to the Pentagon by General Twining, Commander of the Air Materiel Command. Its subject was 'flying discs' and in it Twining said: 'The phenomenon reported is something real and not visionary or fictitious.' And a flight log from July 1947 records the fact that Twining had flown to New Mexico on 7 July. According to Eisenhower's briefing paper, that same day 'a secret operation was begun to assure recovery of the wreckage... for scientific study'.

Forrestal, Bush and Twining were all members of MJ-12. But Joe Nickell, writer for *Skeptical Enquirer* magazine and expert in document analysis, is not convinced.

'It is not what is correct that matters nearly so much as what is wrong,' he says. 'Even a novice forger can be expected to get some things right.'

Nickell's examination of the format and presentation of the documents brought to light a number of serious problems. Although

Truman's signature on the memo to Forrestal matches those on other documents that Truman signed and that are known to be authentic, Nickell points out that it is positioned wrongly on the page. The typefaces, date formats, and style of language used in the MJ-12 papers does not match those in comparable documents from the same sources.

'The many anomalous and suspicious elements detected in the MJ-12 papers clearly demonstrate the documents are forgeries,' Nickell concludes.

Critics also point out that Eisenhower was Army Chief of Staff at the time of the Roswell incident, so he would not have needed to be briefed on the crash. However, the preparation of such briefing papers is common practice in the White House when the adminis-tration changes.

Stanton Friedman dismisses such niggles. His ten years of research have led him to conclude that the papers are genuine.

'Frankly, I consider this ensemble of documents [to be] the most important classified documents ever leaked to the public,' Friedman says. 'I have yet to hear a convincing argument against MJ-12.'

Copies of the MJ-12 documents were sent to British UFO expert Timothy Good. However he became suspicious because Truman's signature on the Forrestal memo was almost identical to one on a memo known to be authentic. No two signatures are the same. Good examined the signature more closely and found a nick on the top of the T that had been whited out. However, he does not dis-miss the documents completely.

'There's definitely something to the documents,' he says. 'If you look at the evidence, there's so much historical [evidence] that's been proved accurate.'

In his 1996 book, *TOP SECRET/MAJIC,* Friedman lists over thirty details not known by anyone outside the government before the film arrived at Jaime Shandera's Hollywood home. Good's con-clusion is that they had been written by a well-informed insider.

'There is such a thing as positive disinformation. These docu-ments could well be that,' he says.

The argument is that even if the documents are fakes they had to be written by someone with inside knowledge who is trying to get the truth to a wider public. Either way the documents prove that the government knows the truth about UFOs and is deliberately covering up.

Canadian Confirmation

The existence of MJ-12 has been alluded to by others in a position to know. In 1950, a Canadian government memo written by defence project engineer Wilbur Smith says: 'Flying saucers exist. Their *modus operandi* is unknown but concentrated effort is being made by a small group headed by Dr Vannevar Bush.'

Former Chairman of the Institute for Defense Analysis Dr Eric Walker recently said that he had known of the existence of MJ-12 for forty years and had attended meetings at Wright–Patterson Air Base in Ohio concerning the recovery of flying saucers. However, former commander of Wright–Patterson Air Base Brigadier General Arthur Exon said he knew nothing of a group called MJ-12. However, he confirmed that there was a top-secret group set up to control access to classified UFO reports. It was called 'The Unholy Thirteen'. UFO enthusiasts have speculated that this was MJ-12 plus one: the President.

Huff and Puff

More information about Majestic-12 came from West Point graduate Bob Huff. After retiring from the US military, he worked as an expert in information technology in companies that were contracted to work for the Federal government and the intelligence community. He has also been investigating the military involvement in the UFO phenomenon for decades.

During the course of his work he was introduced to a former Majestic-12 contractor, whom he calls SARGON, who spilled the beans on the organisation's covert operations. According to Huff, MJ-12 is a government programme that interacts with at least one species of extraterrestrial, either through radio or live interactions. It started in 1947, after the Roswell incident. MJ-12 missions are designed to manage our interactions with the aliens and to exploit reverse-engineering technology for national purposes. Although it acts autonomously, MJ-12 ultimately reports to a joint committee whose members include the directors of both the CIA and the NSA. Boeing, Lockheed, TASC and TRW are all MJ-12 contractors. MJ-12 also has a unique system of identifying potential employees and tracking their careers.

Birdland

The existence of Majestic-12 was again confirmed during the course of a US television documentary aired in October 1988 called *UFO Cover-up? Live*. Two US intelligence agents, whose faces were hidden and whose voices were electronically manipulated to protect their identities, talked openly about its function as a policy-making group on UFO activity. The government knew far more about alien visitations than they were letting on, they said. Then they dropped the bombshell. They revealed that the US government had captured extraterrestrials and learned to communicate with them. One of them, a mechanic from the Zeta Reticuli star system, had even learnt to speak English.

If viewers were unconvinced by this, they filled in all the details. They explained how the aliens love strawberry ice-cream and 'Tibetan-style music'.

The two agents were known only as 'Condor' and 'Falcon' and their story can be traced back to 1979 or 1980. It was then that a 'well-placed individual within the intelligence community' made contact with former Air Force Office of Special Investigations agent and UFOlogist Bill Moore. Moore's shady contact asked him to befriend UFO researcher Paul Bennewitz. Bennewitz was something of an electronics whiz. He lived near Kirtland Air Force Base at Albuquerque, New Mexico – home of the Scandia National Laboratories where military scientists keep watch on the skies using the Starfire laser telescope – and had been attempting to intercept radio signals from it that he believed contained information about UFOs and aliens.

Moore monitored Bennewitz's activities and reported back to

his intelligence contact. Meanwhile his intelligence contact gave him information about aliens to feed to Bennewitz. Although Moore denies it, some of this appears to have been disinformation so that, if Bennewitz published anything he had learnt from his intercepts of Kirtland's communications traffic, he could easily be discredited. What Moore got out of the deal is unclear, but many UFOlogists believe that it was copies of the famous Majestic-12 papers.

Moore maintained communication with his mysterious contact, who began leaking him details of official UFO research. Soon the leak became a flood. It was more than Moore could handle alone so, in 1982, he turned for help to fellow UFOlogist Jaime Shandera. It became clear to Shandera that, if they were to continue to use Moore's contact, they had to use a codename to protect the man's identity. The codename they chose was Falcon.

While Shandera and Moore tried to verify the material Falcon was feeding them, they came across a number of other intelligence insiders who were willing to leak information on the government's involvement with crashed saucers and extraterrestrials. Each was given a bird's name and soon Shandera and Moore were referring to this dissident group of insiders as the 'Aviary'.

Shandera and Moore have never revealed who their contacts were, but other researchers believe they can identify the members of the Aviary. One of them was Bruce Maccabee, an optical physicist and laser weapons expert from the US Naval Surface Weapons Laboratory at Maryland, who used the codename Seagull. Mind-control operations specialist John Alexander, a former colonel from the US Army Intelligence and Security Command and expert in non-lethal weapons, was Penguin. And the CIA's Deputy Director for the Science and Technology Division – the so-called 'weird desk' – Ron Pandolphi was Pelican.

However, a growing number of UFOlogists believe there is more to the Aviary than a random selection of government insiders who want the truth about UFOs and alien encounters to be available to the public at large. And it is thought that Shandera and Moore are pawns in larger game.

Conspiracies Within Conspiracies

Many of the members of the Aviary are senior individuals with extremely high security clearances who have been involved in the UFO investigations on the inside since the early 1970s. They are involved in a political struggle against Majestic who, because of the secrecy surrounding the UFO issue, have formed a government within the government. There is even some overlap between the Aviary and Majestic as MJ-12 have infiltrated the Aviary to keep it under control, or possibly the other way round.

In the meantime, Richard Boylan, author of *Labored Journey to the Stars,* believes that Aviary members are pooling their information in an attempt to 'see the big picture about UFOs and ET contacts with Earth, and to use this privileged information pool to gain access to additional secret data [and] to understand the policies of the elite, hypersecret... group'.

Boylan also believes that there was a split in the Aviary caused by a disagreement between 'lower' level associates who wanted to make UFO information public and the MJ-12 members who wanted to keep it under wraps.

But the conspiracy goes deeper than that. Some of the Aviary members are involved in 'black ops' – projects that are so highly classified that they have no official budgets and are, consequently, not open to Congressional scrutiny. Conspiracy researcher Armen Victorian believes that Aviary members involved in 'black ops' secretly manipulated the group's lower ranking members. They also created alternate levels of UFO cover stories and counter cover stories to cloak their black operations in a mantle of disinformation. According to Victorian: 'Hoaxed and bogus documents suddenly flooded the UFO field and gullible researchers entered into lengthy arguments among themselves, allowing the main proponents behind this well-organised disinformation campaign to further their original work unhindered.'

Certainly members of the Aviary are in key positions and are closely interconnected. For example, Christopher 'Kit' Green – Bluejay – became chief of Biomedical Sciences. Before that, he was the CIA liaison officer for a remote viewing project where he worked with Stanford University's Harold 'Hal' Putholf – Owl – who moved on to the Institute of Advanced Research in Austin, Texas. Another Aviary member, psychic warfare expert Albert Stubblebine – Heron – later headed up the military side of remote viewing. Green also manned the 'weird desk' at the CIA's Division of Science and Technology, the post taken over by Pelican, Ron Pandolphi. Pandolphi also worked at the White House on a project funded by the Rockefeller Foundation to oversee the release of UFO information to the public. That project also involved Commander C.C. Scott Jones – Hummingbird – a retired US Navy officer who served in the Office of Naval Intelligence and went on to become President of the Human Potential Foundation.

Penguin, John Raven, is another key player in the psychic spies projects and was also involved with psychotronic and mind-control research, as was Jack Vorona, who is thought to be Raven – though other candidates include Henry Kissinger, former National Security Advisor Brent Scrowcroft, and Eward Teller, father of the hydrogen bomb.

Then there is Ernie Kellerstraus – Hawk – who has security clearance to handle classified UFO material, worked at Wright–Patterson AFB during the 1970s, and reputedly lived with an ET; Rosemary Guiley – Mourning Dove – director of the US crop circle research group; Barry Hennessy – Bird Colonel – former head of AFOSI; and Jaques Vallee – Partridge – US Defense Department computer expert, former UFO investigator for the French government and prolific writer on UFOs.

Condor is USAF Captain Robert Collins, a former special agent at AFOSI who has been engaged in high-level UFO intelligence operations. No one knows who Falcon is. But there are two candidates: one is Richard Doty – also know as Sparrow – formerly with AFOSI and who went on to become a state policeman in Dulce, New Mexico. The other is Hummingbird, Scott Jones.

Innocent Explanation

Scott Jones freely admits that there was such an organisation as the

Aviary, which tried to encourage the US government to come clean on the UFO issue. But he said that there were no formal meetings as such. He used to meet with other guys who found out that he had a bird name, but he never saw it as an institution.

He was picked to be a member of the Aviary because he had worked in Naval Intelligence for fifteen years and the organisers thought that that would have brought him closer to the truth. However, he never saw any documents relating to the UFOs. Either they did not exist, or he was denied access to them. The evidence he has seen from other, public sources does not impress him, though he believes that extraterrestrial intelligence is impinging on us.

The others in the Aviary, he says, are also keen to get their hands on the evidence. But he can see why the government would be covering up. If they have spent over fifty years since Roswell trying to back-engineer a flying saucer and have still got nowhere, that would be an embarrassment. The Aviary, he says, has not met up for years, though some old friends have stayed in touch.

The Golden Age Dawns

The Majestic-12 committee set up a programme for the systematic study of UFO activity. It began as Project Sign in 1947. Its code-name was changed in 1949 to Grudge, then to Blue Book in 1952. The third phase, Blue Book, shut up shop 1969. By and large, the US government's investigations have been secretive and desultory. However, during that time, there was a golden age of UFO investigation. It was sparked by an incident that occurred at the Army Signal Corps radar centre in Fort Monmouth, New Jersey, on 10 September 1951.

A group of officers were making an inspection of the facility, when a student radar operator picked up an anomalous blip on his radar screen. The contact appeared to be around seven miles to the south-east of the radar station. It was travelling northwards up the coast – and it was travelling too fast to be tracked automatically by the centre's radar, so the operator switched to manual.

The officers watched over the student's shoulder for about three

minutes, until the blip disappeared from the screen. It was travelling in a north-easterly direction at an estimated range of 15,000
yards. The operator estimated that it was travelling at more than
seven hundred miles an hour, faster than the fastest jets in those
days.

Twenty-five minutes after the radar sighting, Lieutenant Wilbert
S. Rogers, in a T-33 Lockheed trainer, pursued as best he could a
silver-coloured disc, flying at around nine hundred miles an hour.
Rogers and his instructor, Major Edward Ballard, dived down at
the object from 20,000 feet, but still could not match its speed. It
was a classic flying saucer, round and flat and between thirty and
fifty feet across. They watched helplessly as the saucer streaked
twenty miles up the coast, before making an extraordinary 120-
degree turn and vanishing over the sea.

The next day, Fort Monmouth radar station tracked two more
high-speed contacts – one at 10:50 a.m., the other at 1:30 p.m. But
it was overcast that day, and there were no planes up to make visual contact.

In the annals of UFOlogy, the Fort Monmouth radar contacts
were unexceptional. However, a report found its way to the office
of Major General Charles Cabell, head of Air Force Intelligence at
the Pentagon. Cabell was intrigued. He ordered a thorough investigation and insisted on being briefed personally on the findings.
Cabell's request landed on the desk of Lieutenant Jerry Cummings
at the Air Technical Intelligence Center in Dayton, Ohio. He had
recently been appointed director of 'Project Grudge', the Air Force
agency assigned to check out UFO reports. When Cummings started to prepare his briefing, he was gratified to discover that the
Monmouth case had already been 'solved' by his team.

'The whole outfit [at Monmouth] were a bunch of young
impressionable kids and the T-33 crew had seen a reflection,' the
Grudge file said. The problem was that analysts had concluded that
without ever leaving their desks in Ohio.

Cummings knew that this was not going to satisfy General
Cabell and turned to his boss, Lieutenant Colonel N. R.
Rosengarten, chief of ATIC's Aircraft and Missiles Branch, for

help. In a matter of hours, they were on their way to New Jersey. The two of them interviewed everyone involved, including Rogers and Ballard. They said that what they had seen was no 'reflection'. They were convinced that it was 'intelligently controlled'. The next morning, Rosengarten and Cummings turned up at the Pentagon to brief Cabell.

When the briefing was over, Cabell wanted to know how Project Grudge was handling its investigations in general. Cummings reported that his men seemed to consider every report as huge joke. This was because the head of ATIC, General Harold Watson, had ordered the staff of Project Grudge to do everything they could to 'degrade the quality of the reports'. Cummings said: 'The only analysis consists of trying to think up new and original explanations that hadn't been sent to Washington before.'

Cabell was furious and complained that he had been lied to. And Rosengarten and Cummings were sent back to Dayton with orders to completely reorganise Project Grudge. Anyone without an open mind, Cabell said, was to be sacked.

Cummings himself was a victim of the reorganisation. He became a civilian and was sent to work on another top-secret government project.

Project Blue Book

Captain Edward J. Ruppelt took over. Project Grudge was redesignated 'Project Blue Book', and given a higher security classification. Channels were established for military personnel to report their UFO sightings directly and more staff were taken on to handle the vastly increased workload. Reports came in so thick and fast that there were never enough people to handle them all. However, high priority cases were routinely investigated in person for the first time. Analysts would no longer be desk-bound debunkers as they had been in the 'Dark Ages'. Under Ruppelt, Blue Book would work like any other military intelligence operation.

To change his staff's thinking on the subject, Ruppelt even coined the term 'Unidentified Flying Object', or 'UFO'. The term

Staff of Project Blue Book, behind Major Hector Quintanilla, Jr.

'flying saucer' was open to ridicule, while a UFO was a serious phenomenon. It was during this period of openness that the Washington flap occurred.

For three consecutive weekends in the summer of 1952, the airspace above Washington, D.C., was buzzing with UFOs. Lights in the night skies were seen by numerous ground and airborne observers, both civilian and military, and contacts filled the capital's radar screens. The Pentagon's switchboards were jammed with calls from the public and ordinary military communications ground to halt. The sightings captured headlines, and the Pentagon held its largest press conference since World War II. In fact, the whole of 1952 was the busiest in Blue Book's history. That year, its analysts investigated over 1,500 cases and 303 cases – some 20 per cent – were designated 'unidentified'.

However, the Washington flap put the wind up the US government. If they could not control the airspace over the capital, what could they control? This was the height of the Cold War; the UFOs presented a clear threat to national security. It undermined the American people's faith in their government. The CIA feared that some foreign power might manipulate the situation to its own advantage. Already, the population of Washington was on the verge of mass hysteria. So they set up the Robertson Panel. It was named after its chairman, the physicist H.P. Robertson, who was head of the Defense Department's Weapons System Evaluation Group and who was also on the CIA's payroll. He recruited other distinguished members, including physicist Samuel A. Goudsmit from the Brookhaven National Laboratories, the winner of the 1968 Nobel prize for physics Luis Alvarez, and astrophysicist Thornton Page, who was deputy director of the Operations Research Office of Johns Hopkins University. They were all prominent sceptics.

They met for two days in Washington in January of 1953 and, instead of calling for a comprehensive and impartial investigation of the phenomenon, they recommended that a programme of serious debunking begin. The media was to be used to strip flying saucers of their mysterious and threatening status. One suggestion was to call in Walt Disney to assist in this, though there is no evidence that he was recruited. The CIA also proposed infiltrating the groups of flying saucer enthusiasts that had sprung up – in case they became the Trojan horse for some foreign power.

The first victim of the new attitude in Washington was Ruppelt. The Cold War was not the right time for open-mindedness, and Ruppelt got his marching orders. When he left the service, he wrote an account of his experiences, *The Report on Unidentified Flying Objects,* which became a classic in the field of UFOlogy.

After Ruppelt, Blue Book was starved of funds. It returned to making desultory desk-bound investigations, half-hearted analysis and debunking. Headed by die-hard sceptics such as Major Hector Quintanilla, it was forced to resort to 'outsourcing', which was handled via the Robertson Panel. A civilian think-tank was instituted to handle a statistical study at the Battelle Memorial Institute. It was codenamed 'Project Stork' and its activities classified. Photographic evidence was handed over to the US Navy Photographic Interpretation Laboratory and the US Air Force

Photo Analysis Division. But despite spending anything up to a thousand hours on some images, they came up with no very firm conclusions.

In 1966, the Air Force handed over its investigation of UFOs to the University of Colorado. Then on 17 December 1969, Blue Book was closed for good. During the two decades of its existence, it had logged 12,618 reports, 701 of which – five per cent – remained unsolved. But in the Ruppelt years, things were very different. In December 1952, Ruppelt briefed the Air Defense Command on 1,021 cases. Some 20.1 per cent could not be accounted for and hoaxes were proved in less than two per cent.

Blue Book was started up again in 1989 as a civilian operation, dedicated to furthering the investigation of the 701 'unidentified' cases.

The Condon Committee

In 1966, the Condon Committee was set up at the University of Colorado by the USAF, under Dr Edward Condon. The Committee comprised a hand-picked bunch of sceptics whose job was to take over the scientific investigation of UFO reports from Blue Book. In 1967, it made its only investigation of an alien abduction case. They did not usually bother with such cases, but were forced to take this one seriously because it involved a police officer.

Dr Edward U. Condon

On 3 December 1967, at around 2:30 a.m., Herbert Schirmer, a patrolman in Ashland, Nebraska was on his way to investigate a livestock disturbance. When he reached a junction, he noticed what at first appeared to be the red taillights of a truck. But when he took a closer look, the truck turned out to be a metallic, flying saucer that was hovering around eight feet above the road. The red lights were coming from portholes around its rim. After a moment, the space ship gave off a fiery glow and shot up into the clouds.

Schirmer returned to the police station thirty minutes later and noted in the station log that he had seen a flying saucer. But when he came to write down the time of the incident, he found that he was unable to account for twenty minutes.

Over the next few days, a red mark appeared on Schirmer's neck. He suffered from splitting headaches and a buzzing in his ears kept him awake at night. These symptoms, he believed, were associated with his encounter.

As the incident was reported by a police officer, it was referred to the Condon Committee. Psychologist R. Leo Sprinkle of the University of Wyoming was also called in. Under regressional hypnosis, Schirmer relived the encounter. This time he recalled that, while he had sat looking mesmerised at the UFO, strange beings approached his car. A green gas had enveloped the car. Then he had passed out. When he came to, Schirmer was being led aboard the spacecraft. It was a friendly enough encounter. He was shown around by a 'grey-skinned being', then he was led back to his car and told to forget all about the encounter.

Sprinkle believed that there was more to it, but although they probed Schirmer, the Condon Committee made it clear that they did not believe a word of it. Schirmer found the stress of the situation too much to handle and quit his job. The Committee promptly dismissed all the evidence that emerged under hypnosis and none of it appeared in their report.

'Unidentified'

One of the very last cases reported to Project Blue Book that was labelled as 'unidentified' occurred in Meridian, Mississippi. Philip Lanning was driving south of town on the evening of 10 July 1967, when his car coasted to a halt and the radio faded. Lanning got out and started to look at the car engine, when an enormous object flew over his head about three hundred feet in the air. The object was silent and moving to the east.

Lanning thought the object was about to crash, but just before the object reached a group of nearby trees, it tilted upward, turned right and then accelerated at great speed straight up into the low-lying clouds. The object was described as being 'like a cymbal on a drum set and was a dirty metallic grey in colour on the under-side'. Lanning saw no portholes or hatches and said that it appeared to the size of house.

Lanning was not sure who would be interested in the report, but he felt that it should be sent to someone in the government, so he forwarded it to a friend in Naval Intelligence. It was handed on to the Air Force. Blue Book eventually received it and began an investigation.

They were impressed with Lanning as a witness, as he was a for-mer military officer who was trained in observation. After exten-sive research and interviews the Air Force were unable to find any conventional explanation and were forced to label this sighting 'unidentified'. This was one of the very last reports in Blue Book to receive that tag.

The Missing Report

Project Blue Book's findings were published in a series of thirteen Blue Book Special Reports. Their overall conclusion was that UFOs did not exist, and that there were no such thing as flying saucers. Sightings could be accounted for in other ways and extra-terrestrials were not paying flying visits to Earth. More specifical-ly: 'No UFO reported, investigated, and evaluated by the Air Force has ever given any indication of a threat to our national security... There has been no evidence indicating that sightings categorised as "unidentified" are extraterrestrial vehicles.' This was the result of the millions of dollars the US government had spent on its official investigations into UFOs.

UFOlogists were naturally disappointed by these conclusions, but that was not the end of the story. Indeed. The Blue Book reports actually posed more questions than they answered. Indeed, one aspect of the publication of the reports themselves cried out for an explanation. If there were thirteen Blue Book reports, how was it possible that the last one was entitled Blue Book Special Report 14? The one before it in the series was Blue Book Special Report 12. What had happened to number thirteen?

The official reason that there was no Special Report 13 was the same reason that American skyscrapers often don't have a thirteenth floor – or that Britain's Ministry of Transport no longer issues car registration plates bearing the number 666, the 'number of the beast'. It is considered bad luck. But surely the people who ran Project Blue Book were rational men who went about their job of examining the evidence for UFOs using scientific methods? These were not the type of people to suffer from triskaidekaphobia – the irrational fear of the number thirteen.

It soon became clear, however, that Blue Book Special Report 13 contained explosive material that the US government did not dare publish. It was, in fact, a repository for all the material that would have caused panic if it had been allowed to get inti the public domain. Then, in the early 1980s, the once water-tight Special Report 13 sprang a leak.

Special Forces

The hole in the dyke came in the form of the tape-recorded testimony of former US Special Forces officer William S. English, the son of an Arizona state senator. In May 1970, he was serving with the Green Berets in Vietnam when he and his A-team were sent on a peculiar mission. They were to make an illegal incursion into neighbouring Laos, locate a Boeing B-52 Stratofortress bomber that had been downed in the triple-canopy jungle there and, if possible, rescue its crew. What was peculiar about this mission was that the B-52 had not been downed by enemy fire. It had crashed after coming off worst in a hostile encounter with a UFO. In tapes of the crew's last Mayday call, they identified their attacker simply as a 'large white light'.

The A-team went into Laos by helicopter and located the B-52. It had not crashed in the normal way, slicing a swathe through the trees on its way down. Instead it lay there, English said, 'like a great big giant hand had grabbed it and just set it down'. The aircraft itself was undamaged. Its bomb load was intact. And there was no damage to the vegetation around it. All the crew were still on board, strapped in their seats. They were all dead and hideously mutilated – but there was no sign of blood. English photographed the grisly scene. Then, following standard army procedures, the team took dog tags from the corpses and buried them in temporary graves, hoping to recover them later. The code books were removed and then the aircraft was blown up.

The mission had spooked English's men. His unit was ambushed in the jungle a few weeks later and most of them were killed. English himself was taken prisoner, but he managed to give his captors the slip and fled into the jungle where he was rescued by US forces some time later. With the American withdrawal from Southeast Asia in 1973, English left the Army. However, he did not leave the service altogether. In 1976 he began working as an intelligence analyst at the major USAF/NSA electronic listening post at RAF Chicksands in Bedfordshire. Chicksands is the home of the USAF's 6950th Electronic Security Group, which monitors and analyses military communications across Europe using the so-called Elephant Cage – a massive ring of radio aerials.

As part of his duties, on 29 June 1976 he was given a 625-page document to assess. It was entitled Grudge/Blue Book Report 13. English says that the report seemed incredible. It contained reports of alien encounters and described the captured extraterrestrial craft, detailing their armaments. There were also autopsy reports on dead aliens. It was unbelievable, except for one incident. Among the close-encounter reports was the report of the downed B-52 English had investigated in Laos. It contained the photographs English himself had taken six years earlier, showing the mutilated crew. This convinced English that the report was genuine. He submitted an assessment saying that, and got on with other work.

English does not know if he had been given the report by accident, but a few weeks later he was summarily dismissed. On the orders of the base commander, Colonel Robert Black, he was shipped back to the US that very day. Bewildered, he found himself dumped back in his hometown, Tucson, Arizona. English could only conclude that his dismissal had something to do with the Blue Book report he had read. This tweaked his interest in UFOs and he went to a lecture given by the well-known UFOlogist Stanton Friedman at Pima Community College. After the lecture, English approached Friedman, who was intimidated at first.

'English is a big man, physically imposing,' says Friedman. 'He looked anxious, like he didn't want to be in one place for too long. Initially he was quite scary until he trusted that I was taking him seriously.'

Then he told Friedman what he had seen. So there could be no dispute later about what he had said, his testimony was tape-recorded, and he told Friedman and the tape recorder all he knew.

English began working as a researcher for the Aerial Phenomena Research Organisation, then one of the top UFO groups, which was based in Tucson. Through APRO he met the astronomer J. Allen Hynek, who had been an advisor to Blue Book and whose hand-written notes were scattered throughout the report. In a private conversation, Hynek confirmed that the report English had evaluated was the missing Grudge 13 report. But Hynek said he would deny this if English went public.

Four years later, Colonel Black and his staff sergeant turned up in Tucson. They told English that they had also been kicked out of the USAF because of the Grudge 13 report. The three men were

James and Coral Lorenzen, founders of APRO (Aerial Phenomena Research Organisation) in 1952.

aggrieved and swore to do something about it. Colonel Black knew just what they should do. He told English that a large alien craft was buried on the White Sands Missile Range in New Mexico. They should mount an expedition to find it. To finance this, English sold the leather-goods business he had started in Tucson to support himself. They bought a van, which they filled with cameras, video recorders and other equipment. Armed with infrared-sensing devices, gravitometers, magnetometers and sound detectors, the intrepid trio broke into the highly restricted White Sands Missile Range.

Naturally, the authorities were not too thrilled about having their security compromised by renegade UFOlogists. When their infiltration was detected, the military sent helicopters, which fired rockets at the van. The van was destroyed and Colonel Black and his staff sergeant, who were in it, were killed. Luckily, English was about half-a-mile away on foot. He managed to escape and headed for the Tucson home of fellow UFO researcher Wendelle Stevens. His own home was under surveillance and English had himself smuggled out of Tucson. Eventually, he settled Lynchburg, Virginia, where he worked for a few years as a TV cameraman.

But the authorities would not leave him alone. In September 1988, he decided that he had nothing to lose by going public. In December 1988, English posted his story on the Internet. It detailed the fifteen attempts that had been made on his life because of his knowledge of Grudge 13. In one attack, two men had raked his Lynchburg home with machine gun fire for fifteen minutes. They fired at least two thousand rounds at the house. The local police precinct was only two hundred yards away, but no came to his help.

As well as government assassins, English has also been the target of debunkers. They point out that, according to Pentagon records, no B-52 was lost in Southeast Asia between July 1969 and July 1972. If a B-52 was downed in the Laotian jungle in April or May 1970, it had been expunged from the official records. A B-52 Stratofortress is a large and costly aircraft, and it is hard to lose one without it being noticed. The histories of all of the B-52s made by Boeing between November 1951 and October 1962 exist. Each one can be accounted for, officially. But it must be remembered that the Vietnam war was fraught with misreporting – overestimating the enemy's body count while under-reporting US loses. As Congress had given the administration no permission to bomb Laos, over-flights by fully laden B-52s were illegal and the loss of a B-52 there would have been covered up.

It has also been said that English was, in fact, too young to have served in Special Forces in 1970. Records show that English did serve in the US Army but as a telephone technician with the rank of Spec 4, or corporal. However, Friedman has checked his military credentials and believes that he has the necessary credentials to see government records on UFO activity.

However, it is unlikely that he served in Southeast Asia in that capacity. The British Home Office has no record of the deportation of a William S. English in 1976, though this would have been a military matter. Records also show that the American base commander of RAF Chicksands from September 1974 until August 1976 was Colonel James W. Johnson Jr. and not Colonel Robert Black. However, if there is a cover-up, the records would be easy to falsify.

Joint Venture

Former Green Beret William English was not the only one to come forward. Milton W. Cooper was a Petty Officer in the US Navy in 1972 when he too saw Grudge 13. He says that it was not released because it details the co-operation between the US government and the aliens. In a joint venture, they are constructing a base on the moon. The aliens are providing the technology while the US government are providing the manpower, in the form of human slaves. The elite are going to start a human colony there after the destruction of the Earth which will happen 'by or soon after the year 2000'.

According to Cooper, another colony is being secretly planned on Mars. He says that on 22 May 1962 a probe landed on the red planet and confirmed the existence of an environment that could support life. This does not even convince fellow UFOlogists.

Stanton Friedman said: 'If Cooper told me it was raining, I'd go and put a pair of shorts on.'

However, although Friedman does not trust Cooper, he does believe that Grudge 13 exists. He finds English's story plausible and says that his description of the report matches that given to him by a military colleague that he won't name. This convinces him that it is real and that it is not being released because the information it contains is explosive.

Disinformation

The existence of Grudge 13 has always been denied by the USAF, who say that the material originally intended for Blue Book Report 13 – the findings of an investigation known as Project Stork – was incorporated in Blue Book 14. Assuming this to be true, some UFOlogists have come up with theories about what was in the Grudge/Blue Book Report 13 that English and others claim to have seen.

'I am not questioning the good faith of their testimony,' says Vallee. 'The documents in question may have been nothing more than fabrications designed by their superiors to test their abilities to screen disinformation. It would only have been natural to test their degree of gullibility and their analytical skill, to thrust under their noses a document that mixed some element of reality with some preposterous claims, as any good piece of good disinformation art would. If that was the case, they certainly did not pass the test.

But then one could accuse Vallee of being part of the disinformation campaign too. Friedman says that certain journalists and researchers ridicule English out of hand because he makes fantastic claims with little evidence to back them up. But the critics have little evidence either, says Friedman: 'This, in itself is the perpetuation of disinformation.

National Security

The USAF has been involved with the UFO phenomenon, and naturally they involved military intelligence. Then in 1952 the CIA got involved, in case the agents of foreign powers infiltrated the UFO community, provoked mass hysteria or simply used sightings to jam the switchboard at the Pentagon. However, another far more shadowy agency was also taking an interest in UFOs.

Of America's thirteen intelligence agencies, the biggest and most secretive is undoubtedly the National Security Agency. While the CIA was set up by Congress and is answerable to the legislators, the NSA was established by Presidential fiat and is answerable only to the chief executive himself.

Founded in 1952, its headquarters are in Fort Meade, Maryland, where it has a staff of 50,000, mainly seconded from the military. It also maintains listening posts in the UK and Japan and other parts of the world. The NSA has two main responsibilities. It is charged with maintaining the security of communications within the US government and protecting them 'against exploitation through interception, unauthorised access, or related technical intelligence threats'. To do this, it is in charge of code making and polices the flow of information in and out of the country.

Its other task involves communications intelligence – COMINT – and electronic intelligence – ELINT. It intercepts telephone calls, faxes and e-mails world-wide and breaks codes. It also monitors the military communications of other nations and eavesdrops on radar and electronic warning systems. Of greater interest to UFOlogists is its role in collecting signals intelligence, known in the military as SIGINT.

Listening in to the entire electromagnetic spectrum, if alien spacecraft were anywhere near the Earth, the NSA would pick up their messages and any signals given off by their control systems. Even if some other agency received the first communication from aliens, it would be handed to the NSA. The agency is in the business of code breaking. It employs the world's top mathematicians, linguists, cryptologists and supercomputers. These would be dedicated to decoding and translating any alien information. So if anyone knows about UFOs, it is the NSA.

Freedom of Information

When the Freedom of Information Act was passed in 1974 in the wake of the Watergate scandal, UFOlogists attempted to use it to force classified UFO information out of America's intelligence agencies. The key player was attorney Peter Gersten, a UFO researcher and legal counsel for Citizens Against UFO Secrecy (CAUS). He discovered that UFO documents given to him by the CIA referred to other files held by the NSA. Then on 9 November 1978, he was given notice that a number of the CIA documents he was after had been sent to the NSA prior to declassification. UFOlogists believe that the CIA was, in fact, leaking the information that the NSA were involved in UFO monitoring. However, when Gersten filed an FOIA request with the NSA, the agency refused to open their files on grounds of national security. But, in doing so, they tacitly admitted that they were holding UFO data in the first place.

On 23 January 1980, CAUS made an another attempt to get the material released. When the NSA refused, CAUS took the case to federal court. On 18 November 1980, Federal Judge Gerhard Gesell upheld the NSA's refusal. So CAUS appealed the following January. This also failed. CAUS then petitioned the Supreme Court in Washington, D.C, but on 8 March 1982, the justices announced their decision not to hear the case.

But during this judicial process, the NSA had to explain to the courts why they had to withhold the information. To do this, the NSA's Director of Policy, Eugene Yeates, issued an *in camera* affidavit to Judge Gesell. This is a sworn affidavit that is lodged with the court in a closed session and its contents themselves are classified. The affidavit outlined the contents of the NSA's classified UFO files and explained why they could not be released to the public. But the only people allowed to read the affidavit were the judge and the NSA's lawyers.

This gave CAUS a new avenue of attack. They filed an FOIA request for 'all or any portion' of Yeates' affidavit. Again, they had to jump through hoops. But in May 1982, they eventually succeeded. The NSA released the affidavit, though 412 of the 582 lines of type handed over had been blacked out by the censor. And the page numbering showed that eleven pages were missing entirely. Plainly the NSA were hiding something.

The remaining 170 lines of the affidavit released explained that: 'The COMINT reports being withheld… are all based on intercepted foreign communications. The disclosure of these records would identify the communications that had been successfully intercepted and processed for intelligence purposes. No meaningful portion of any of the records could be segregated and released without identifying the communications underlying the communications intelligence report… Disclosing them would permit foreign intelligence officials to draw inferences [and] to take countermeasures… to defeat the capabilities of NSA's intelligence gathering techniques.'

Even the least paranoid of UFO researches who normally had no truck with conspiracy theories believed that the NSA were hiding something and they were refusing to release documents, not for reasons of NSA procedure but precisely because of their UFO content. Meanwhile, the NSA continued their blanket denials.

'Regarding your enquiry about UFOs, please be advised that the NSA do not have any interest in UFOs in any manner,' one NSA information officer told UFO researcher Robert Todd, even though the declassified affidavit revealed that the NSA had 156 classified UFO files.

Stanton Friedman took to waving the blacked-out affidavit about at his lectures and on TV appearances, calling the NSA's cover-up a 'Cosmic Watergate'. Meanwhile, other researchers became convinced that the NSA was refusing to release the documents because they proved that the US government was in contact with aliens. Even sceptics were unhappy about the NSA's handling of the situation. It seemed to have been playing into the hands of the most radical in the UFO community.

Declassification

In late 1996, the NSA decided to change its stance. It released a less censored version of the blacked-out affidavit lodged with Judge Gesell. Only 30 per cent of the original affidavit was readable; now only 25 cent was blacked out. The agency also began to declassify many of the 156 files it had withheld in 1982. Interestingly, among the first to receive copies of the declassified material was veteran UFO debunker Philip Klass. In January 1997, he published selections in his *Skeptics UFO Newsletter*.

The documents were, of course, innocuous. They were intercepts of Soviet air defence messages transmitted from radar stations sent between 1958 and 1979. These would obviously have been of interest to the USAF's Strategic Air Command. They still contained blacked-out sections, but these seemed to hide the locations of the installations, the names of agents and clues to the NSA's intercept capabilities. So a typical report reads:

'[censored] unidentified flying object (UFO): (A) 0028-0325, four UFO (probably balloon) moved slowly from SE of [censored] towards SW and passed [censored]. (B) 0325-0515, one UFO (probably a balloon) moved slowly from [censored] toward west, passed [censored] and faded [censored]... (D) 1355-1630, 19 UFO (probably balloons) moved from [censored] and [censored] towards west and faded [censored] and [censored], alt 69,000-79,000ft. [censored]'

According to the NSA, the UFOs mentioned in these reports are – like all sightings in the UK and US – probably balloons. NSA analysts say that the Soviets attached radar reflectors to balloons and released them secretly to check their height-finding radars and their radar operators' performance. The groups of figures – such as 1355-1630 – refer to the time during which contact with UFO remained on the screen. The slow progress of these objects confirms that they are balloons, the NSA say. It can, of course, be argued that the NSA had fourteen years to collect innocent intercepts to release – and why were they not released immediately after the collapse of the Soviet Union in 1991?

Insider's Story

Former NSA agent Thomas P. Deuley was working in the communications section of the NSA when the CAUS FOIA request arrived. He had been working there for about two years and, as a

UFO enthusiast, he had collected about two-thirds of a file drawer full of material. He photocopied it all and sent it to the NSA's FOIA office. However, he says that only some of it was actually classified. He did not have the signals intelligence data. What he had were largely clippings of magazines and newspapers and sightings reports. He does not know of any other material, though he does believe that there have been a few genuine UFO incidents, but he is sure that the government is not involved and does not know how they would keep such a thing hushed up.

Cuban Crisis

There is one genuine incident that the NSA was involved in, which took place in 1978. It is mentioned in the NSA papers, though many of the details are heavily censored. According to Stanton Friedman, the full story is that an intelligence analyst from the USAF's 6947 security squadron intercepted a message from a Cuban radar station, saying that it had picked up a UFO flying at 750 miles an hour at 98,000 feet. Two MiG-21 jet fighters were scrambled. They made visual contact and reported seeing a 'bright metallic sphere with no visible markings or appendages'. They tried to hail it by radio but failed to make contact. Then they were ordered to destroy it. The flight leader got his weapons system locked on to the object, but before he could fire his aircraft disintegrated. The NSA had all tapes and reports of the incident shipped to Fort Meade and made an official note that the Cuban MiG had been lost 'due to equipment malfunction'. When confronted with the details of this case, the NSA can only answer lamely: 'The factual circumstances of the incident reported in this record… are considered to be fictitious.'

Soviet Sightings

Even in the Soviet intercepts released by the NSA, the evidence of extraterrestrial activity comes through. One report says: '[censored] sights UFO [censored] sighted a UFO described as spherical or disc-like in form with no established color, brighter than the sun, with a diameter of one-half the visible size of the moon. At the time of observation, object was at the upper edge of the clouds on a true bearing 120 degrees, azimuth 080 degrees travelling north.'

Another says: '[censored] sight three unidentified flying objects [censored] at 1915 [censored], three luminous objects were seen in the western part of [censored]. The first object was shaped like a horseshoe and was white in color. The other two were round and yellow in color.' So they are out there.

Ignorance is Bliss

While the Americans have developed all sorts of sophisticated conspiracies to cover up what the government knows about their extra-terrestrial involvements, the British are altogether more amateurish. Take, for example, the incident that occurred on 5 November 1990. That day a squadron of Royal Air Force Tornadoes was flying over the North Sea on its way back to base. Suddenly, a high-speed UFO streaked past them. The pilots were amazed at its speed and none of the trained observers was able to identify the craft. Nevertheless, the squadron signalled the Ministry of Defence with a report of the encounter.

However, when they landed they were not met with intelligence officers eager to debrief them about what they had seen. Nor were they visited by the menacing 'Men in Black'. No one told them to keep quiet about the incident, nor were they threatened with prose-cution under the Official Secrets Act if they opened their mouth about it down the pub that night. Instead, the MoD used its tried and tested way of dealing with awkward UFO sightings. It sent the pilots' signal to the division in charge of investigating UFO reports. There the report was marked 'Object unexplained: case closed'. Then this was filed along with all the other sighting reports. And that was the end of the matter.

The British have not always been so blasé about UFOs. An official report of sorts was prepared in 1951. It has since disappeared, but there is a reference to it in a letter dated 9 August 1952 from the Air Ministry to Prime Minister Winston Churchill. He had asked for the study to be carried out. Its conclusion, it seems, was that all UFOs could be explained in conventional terms. However, how much original work went into the study is not known. It certainly relied heavily on the information that had been amassed by the USAF's Projects Sign, Grudge and Blue Book since 1947.

Captain Edward J. Ruppelt, who headed Grudge and Blue Book between 1951 and 1953, was contacted by the British. In his 1956 book *The Report On Unidentified Flying Objects*, Ruppelt revealed that he had been visited by two RAF intelligence officers. They arrived at the headquarters of Project Blue Book with six sheets of questions. The answers Ruppelt gave provided the basis for their report and its seems very likely that no other work was done before an answer was given to Churchill.

Although Churchill had some interest in UFOs in 1912, in the 1950s he was more concerned that the sightings of high-speed flying craft were a new type of Soviet aircraft that was being used to probe Britain's air defences. The Cold War was at its height and the British military were more interested in enemies invading their airspace than extraterrestrials. Extraterrestrials represented a negligible threat, compare to the massed nuclear-armed strike force of the Soviet Air Force. Alien craft were a distraction. There was no point on wasting over-stretched manpower on them. So sightings were filed and forgotten. Not only were the files closed, the minds were closed, too.

The attitude the British government adopted was revealed in a letter dated 24 June 1965. The letter was a reply to an enquiry by the Department of the Air Force in Washington, D.C. In it, the MoD outlined their policy. It was 'to play down the subject of UFOs and to avoid attaching undue attention or publicity to it'. The British establishment took a conservative view and regarded investigating UFO sightings as a huge waste of time.

Not all the military are total sceptics though. Lord Hill-Norton, Admiral of the Fleet and Chief of the Defence Staff from 1971 to 1973, is convinced that UFOs pose a potential threat. As a member of the House of Lords' All-Party UFO study group, he pressed the military establishment to take the threat seriously.

Along with other government documents, UFO files are subject to the thirty-year rule. Unless the government feel that the information is particularly sensitive, all government files are open for viewing at the Public Record Office in Kew after thirty years. It is clear from the documents that have been released that there have been numerous UFO encounters in British air space. They have been seen by military witnesses and detected on radar. In many cases, RAF jets were scrambled to intercept the UFOs, usually unsuccessfully. Some ten per cent of sightings remain unexplained, and the MoD has acknowledged that these cases defy explanation, even in the rare case that there has been a rigorous investigation. But by and large these secret files reveal that, in most of these cases, no further action was taken once the encounter itself had been reported – even when jet fighters had been scrambled to intercept the intruders.

This lack of follow-up is exactly what happened in the well-attested Rendlesham Forest UFO incident in December 1980. Lieutenant Colonel Halt submitted a remarkable report to the MoD about UFO activity near the military bases of RAF Bentwaters and RAF Woodbridge. The report told how abnormally high radiation readings had been taken at a site where a small, metallic UFO had been seen to land. However, the MoD never even acknowledged that it had received Halt's memorandum and certainly nothing was done about it. The MoD's policy, like that of the British government as a whole, is that it is better to keep your head in the sand, and they reply to all enquiries by saying: 'To date, no evidence of any threat to the United Kingdom has been found.'

Rudloe Manor

There are some that believe that the attitude of the British government is not just driven by incompetence and indifference. In his book *A Covert Agenda*, Nick Redfern points to the involvement of the Provost and Security Services, a wing of the RAF that deals with security vetting and counter-intelligence. While the MoD have consistently denied that they have any role in UFO investigation, Redfern unearthed a document in the Public Record Office from 1962 that proved otherwise. And he got a letter from Group Captain Rose at RAF Rudloe Manor in Wiltshire confirming it.

Many British UFOlogists believe that Rudloe Manor is the centre of secret UFO research. UFO researcher Timothy Good was arrested by military policemen when walking around the perimeter of the base. Later he was encouraged to telephone in a UFO sighting report to Rudloe Manor by Ralph Noyes, former head of Defence Sectretariat 8 – the forerunner of Secretariat (Air Staff) 2a. Noyes is now a leading authority on UFOs and crop circles and he wanted to see if staff at Rudloe Manor would accept the sighting report. They did – though nothing further happened.

Redfern believes that the MoD do realise that something very strange is going on, but they don't know what to do about it. If they admit that they don't have all the answers, they appear foolish and vulnerable – the last thing you want from the military. They are powerless, Redfern says, so they have no choice but to cover up.

Police Business

Although it is the military that is officially charged with investigating UFO sightings, it is often the police who make first contact with UFO eyewitnesses or aliens themselves. Unfortunately, official scepticism is also rife in the police – even when it is a police officer who had the encounter.

At 5:45 p.m. on the afternoon of Friday, 24 April 1964, Patrolman Lonnie Zamora was hot on the heels of a speeding black Chevrolet near Socorro, New Mexico. It was sunny day. Suddenly Zamora saw a flame in the sky and heard a loud roaring noise. The patrolman thought that a miner's dynamite shack had blown up. He broke off the chase and headed instead towards the mysterious flame to see if anyone was hurt.

As Zamora turned off the highway, down the rough gravel road towards the dynamite shack, he noticed a shiny, metallic object in a gulch some 250 yards to the south. He stopped his patrol car and got out. The object looked like an overturned car. Next to it he saw two small figures in white cover-alls, which he took to be children, and he assumed they were responsible.

Zamora got back into his patrol car and drove towards the scene. As he did so, he reported back to the sheriff's office in Socorro by radio, giving them the location in case he needed back-up. He pulled up about thirty yards away. As he opened the car door to get out, he heard another loud roar. It was then that he realised that the metallic object was not a car at all. Flames belched from underneath it and the object rose slowly, vertically, into the air. The object was egg-shaped and aluminium coloured, with red markings around its middle that looked like some sort of insignia. It had no windows, doors or other external features. However, it did seem to have slanted legs on the underside, which Zamora took to be landing gear.

As the strange craft rose higher, Zamora could see a blue and orange flame spewing from a port in the middle of its underside. It produced no smoke, but the exhaust kicked up dust in the immediate area. As the roar increased, Zamora feared the object might blow up and he ran for safety behind a hillock. But, before he got there, he noticed that the roaring had stopped, so he ducked down behind a bush. The craft had risen some fifteen feet, and it then shot off horizontally, narrowly missing the dynamite shack. Zamora watched as it headed off south-east.

He ran back to his car and radioed in, keeping an eye on the UFO as it flew away.

'Look out the window and tell me what you see,' he told the police radio officer Ned Lopez.

'What am I looking for?' asked Lopez.

'It looks like a balloon,' said Zamora. But by that time the object had climbed to an enormous height and soon disappeared into the distance.

New Mexico State Trooper Sergeant M. Samuel Chavez was despatched to assist Zamora. As he waited, Zamora made a sketch of the insignia he had seen on the side of the UFO. Then he went back down to the scene where the brush was on fire in several places.

When Chavez arrived, he noted that Zamora looked pale and sweaty.

'You look like you've seen the devil,' he said.

'Maybe I have,' said Zamora.

He told Chavez what had happened. Then the two officers

looked around the gulch where Zamora had seen the object on the ground. They found that the earth was scorched and a bush was still smouldering. Chavez also found four wedge-shaped imprints in the middle of the burned area. Being a sceptic by nature, Chavez later took a surreptitious look in Zamora's car, searching for implements that Zamora might have used to fake these landing marks. He found nothing.

Undersheriff James Luckie and State Policeman Ted Jordan turned up to photograph and search the scene. At 7 p.m., Zamora and Chavez returned to the precinct. FBI agent J. Arthur Byrnes happened to be there on other business. He heard about the incident on the police radio and waited to talk to the two men. Byrnes then called the local army base and spoke to Captain Richard T. Holder. Twenty minutes later, Holder arrived at the station and sat in while Byrnes formally interviewed Zamora. When he had heard Zamora's story, Byrnes told Zamora that it would be better for all concerned if he did not mention the two small figures he had seen dressed in white, as no one would believe him.

Then, with a team of Socorro police officers, Byrnes and Holder visited the site. Concerned by what he had seen, Holder called in the military police. They roped off the scene. It was now dark so, with the aid of flashlights, they collected samples and made measurements. It was 1 a.m. before Holder completed his report and sent it to Washington. Then he waited.

Later that morning Holder got a call from a colonel from the Pentagon war room of the Joint Chiefs of Staff. Over a scrambled line he asked Holder to give him a personal briefing. The Air Force investigation began immediately. There was no time to lose. The story had already hit the newswires. Reporters were calling Major Hector Quintanilla, then head of the Project Blue Book, non-stop, though he refused to speak to them.

Quintanilla flew to New Mexico and had the site checked for radioactivity, but there were no unusual readings. Blue Book investigators checked the radar records, but found no unusual contact in the area at the time. Meanwhile, the soil samples Holder had taken were sent to the Air Force Materials Laboratory for spectographic analysis. No traces of non-terrestrial materials were found. The investigation was getting nowhere, so Quintanilla sent for Project Blue Book's scientific consultant, astronomer J. Allen Hynek.

Hynek flew to New Mexico. At Socorro, he got Zamora to take him to the site of the encounter and talk him through the whole incident. He then examined the site for himself but found no new evidence. Hynek deduced that, if the encounter was a hoax, Zamora must be in on it. So he cross-questioned Zamora again, hoping to find something that would invalidate his testimony. But he could not shake the patrolman's story.

Hynek announced his conclusions at a press conference.

'It is my opinion that a real, physical event occurred on the out-skirts of Socorro that afternoon,' Hynek said.

Quintanilla was furious at Hynek for adding fuel to the fire, but he too believed that Zamora had seen a real physical craft that afternoon. However, he believed it was man-made. He checked out nearby Holloman Air Force Base, but they were testing no new equipment there that might account for Zamora's sighting. He later thought that a lunar lander might fit the bill. He contacted NASA and asked whether they were testing them in the field.

The concept of the lander had been developed in late 1962. NASA signed a contract with the manufacturer on 14 January 1963. Over the next three months, the design of the prototype was drawn up. Testing was planned for New Mexico. But as it turned out, the lunar landing modules were not operational in April 1964, when Zamora made his sighting. Besides, the lunar lander was dis-tinctly not egg-shaped. It had no reason to be streamlined as there is no atmosphere on the moon. Reluctantly, Quintanilla was forced to conclude that the case justified the label 'unidentified'.

Independent Enquiries

UFOlogists were already suspicious of the military's debunking of UFO cases so, on Sunday, 26 April, Jim and Coral Lorenzen of the Aerial Phenomena Research Organisation in Tucson, Arizona, drove to Socorro to conduct their own investigation. The first thing they did was look at the marks that had been left on the ground. The

UFO's legs, they found, had left wedge-shaped impressions, three to four inches deep. The span between them was around ten feet. They also found four circular depressions, some three inches deep and four inches in diameter. These, they assumed, had been left by the ladder that the small alien figures Zamora had seen used to get in and out of the ship. And on the exact spot where Zamora had seen the small figures standing, they found four small prints with a little crescent shape in the middle. They could only conclude that these were the aliens' footprints.

But the Lorenzens did not have the field to themselves. On Tuesday, 28 April, Ray Stanford, a psychic who has seen UFOs many times himself, turned up. He was an investigator for the National Investigations Committee on Aerial Phenomena, a high-profile UFO group based in Washington, D.C, and run by retired Marine Major Donald E. Keyhoe. He talked to Zamora and discovered that Captain Holder had told him not to mention the insignia he had seen on the side of the craft, except to official investigators, and FBI agent Byrnes had told him not to mention the two small figures he had seen. He later discovered that Byrnes had asked to have his name removed from the case.

When he examined the site, he found metallic scrapings on a rock in one of the depressions in the soil where the object had stood. He collected these and sent them for analysis at the Goddard Space Flight Center in Greenbelt, Maryland. Stanford was told initially that the scrapings were of a zinc-iron alloy unknown on Earth. This proved that the object that Zamora had seen at Socorro was of extraterrestrial origin. However, the scientists who did the analysis subsequently said the samples were simply sand.

Standford was later told by James McDonald, a senior atmospheric physicist at the University of Arizona, that a radiological chemist working for the Public Health Service in Las Vegas had analysed other material collected at the site. This included vitrified sand collected at Socorro. However, the chemist's notes and samples were confiscated by the Air Force. USAF personnel had also taken State Patrolman Ted Jordan's photographs. When he asked for them back, he was told that the film had been ruined – apparently it had been irradiated.

However, this did not take the investigation much further forward. Work on it effectively ended right there. Local people in Socorro thought that the object Zamora had seen was probably a secret experimental device. The flame from its engine made it seem very much like a terrestrial object. The regular excuse, that the object was a hot-air balloon – there was a balloon race in the area at the time – was trotted out. And UFO debunker Donald Menzel said that Zamora was the victim of a prank.

But Zamora is clear in his mind what he saw that day. It was not some secret experimental craft, a vertical take-off and landing aircraft, or a hot air balloon.

'I know what I saw,' he says, 'and it wasn't any of those.'

The Socorro incident remained as Project Blue Book's only 'unidentified' case that involved the sighting of a UFO and its occupants on the ground, though Quintanilla felt that the real 'solution to this case could very well be lying dormant in Lonnie Zamora's head'. And for the UFO community, it is the first solid case of a close encounter of the third kind.

The year after the Socorro encounter, the scientific community began looking for a site to build the VLA – Very Large Array – the world's largest radio telescope. In 1972, they decided to build it, of all places, at Socorro. In 1975, the first dish-shaped antenna was erected. It would be the first of twenty-seven arranged in a huge Y shape over twenty miles across. This VLA has been used by SETI – the Search for Extraterrestrial Intelligence – and is the very place that the first alien communication is received in Carl Sagan's ground-breaking novel *Contact*.

Lavender Vandals

The following year a similar sighting took place in France. In 1965, Maurice Masse, a farmer living in Valensole, France, was having problems with his lavender crop. Over several weeks he had found bare patches in the crops which he could not account for. Then one morning in July at around 6 a.m., he noticed what he thought were two boys playing in the field. He immediately concluded that he had found the culprits who were responsible for destroying his lavender crop.

As he made off after them, he noticed a strange craft which he took to be a peculiar sort of helicopter. The 'boys' were making towards it. As Maurice caught up with them he realised that they were not boys at all. In fact, they were not human, but instead strange looking beings, with large bald heads, pasty faces and huge slanted eyes. They wore one-piece cover-alls, and one had a tube-like instrument by his side.

The alien lifted this tubular device, pointed it at the advancing Maurice and shot a ray of light at him. This knocked him to the ground and he lay there paralysed for several minutes. When he was able to move again, he saw the craft shoot vertically up into the sky at a tremendous speed.

When he was later shown an artist's impression of the craft that Lonnie Zamora had seen at Socorro, he said: 'Someone else has seen my UFO.' The lavender has never grown back on the spot where the UFO landed.

Interpretation of a UFO event by artist Michael Buhler, Valensole, France

The Long Arm of the Law

Aliens do not have run-ins with the law only in the United States. At 3:15 a.m., on 13 March 1997, local policemen Anerilton Neves and Moacir Pereira dos Santos were driving through the deserted streets of the Nations Park district of the city of Americana near Sao Paulo, Brazil. It was a quiet night and the two officers were on their way to the precinct. Then, as they reached the intersection of Malaysia Street and United States Avenue, they saw a dazzling light appear in the skies ahead of them.

They pulled over and got out to take a closer look. The light came from an object hovering about six hundred feet above the road. It was oval, with red, blue and yellow lights around it. As the two officers watched, the UFO moved noiselessly off over an area of wasteland. Dos Santos ran back to the patrol car and flicked on the car's emergency lights. Immediately, the UFO shot away into the night sky. As it disappeared, they could see that its lights formed a triangle.

A few moments later, local taxi driver Henrique Moretti pulled up. He and his terrified passenger had just seen a UFO. It was about fifteen feet across and hovered some five hundred feet above the cab, before shooting off noiselessly in the direction of the nearby town of Nova Odessa.

Neves and dos Santos called Americana Police Central Control and requested assistance. When more policemen turned up at the scene, they laughed at Neves and dos Santos's stories. Their eyes had been playing tricks on them. But when Moretti and his passenger said that they had also seen the UFO, the laughter stopped. It soon became clear that they were not the only ones to have seen it. Numerous reports of sightings came in from all over the city. Indeed, two other policemen had seen it, along with a radio announcer and a photographer who had managed to photograph it. When the case was investigated, the Brazilian Air Force reported that they had not been airborne that night and the Brazilian National Institute of Space Research said that no meteorological experiments involving balloons or any other airborne objects had been undertaken on the evening of the sighting. The case remains officially 'unresolved'.

The Police in Force

On 17 April 1966, Deputy Sheriff Dale F. Spaur and his deputy, Wilbur Neff, were out on night patrol in Portage County, Ohio. At 4:45 a.m., they were sent to visit a woman who lived in the west of the county. She had reported seeing a bright object, 'as big as a house' fly over her neighbourhood and she was highly agitated.

Puzzled, Spaur and Neff set off to investigate the case. The woman had little to add and the patrolmen set about a routine inspection of the area. While they were investigating a car parked illegally nearby, Spaur noticed a strange object hovering over the neighbouring woods. It was so low that the patrolmen did not see it until it was practically on top of them. The only sound it made was a slight hum, but the light it gave off was so intense that the patrolmen looked down at their clothes to check if they were on fire. The huge cone-shaped UFO hovered over them for some time before moving off to the east.

Back in the patrol car, Spaur radioed in his sighting of a 'bright object' in the sky and received orders to shoot at it. So Spaur and Neff flicked on the siren and gave chase.

Fellow officer Wayne Huston, who was patrolling some twenty-five miles to the east, saw the UFO streak past at a speed of around fifty miles an hour. Huston described it as 'shaped like an ice cream cone with a sort of partly melted down top'. When Spaur and Neff came down the road after it, Huston fell in behind. They headed off on a fifty-mile chase at speeds of up to eighty miles an hour.

Over the border in Conway, Pennsylvania, Officer Frank Panzanella was heading down Second Avenue at 5:20 a.m. when he saw a bright shiny object flying by. He got out of the car and was looking at it when Spaur and Neff's, and then Huston's, black-and-whites pulled up. All four officers then watched agog as the object stopped, rose up, flew off to the left of the moon and vanished. Another officer, Gerald Buchert, saw the UFO and managed to photograph it, but he was forbidden to publicise his pictures.

Despite this incredible story, Major Hector Quintanilla, then head of the Air Force's Project Blue Book, dismissed the eyewitness testimony of five police officers. He concluded that they had first seen a satellite, then transferred their gaze to the planet Venus. But Blue Book's scientific consultant J. Allen Hynek disgreed.

'A more lucid example of the disregarding of evidence unfavourable to a preconceived explanation could hardly be found,' he said.

Bobbies on the Beat

At around 2:30 a.m., one January morning in 1978, Sergeant Tony Dodd and Police Constable Alan Dale were driving near the town of Cononley, North Yorkshire, when the dark country lane in front of them was suddenly lit by a mysterious light. As they travelled towards it, they experienced heavy static on their police radio. When they stopped the car to investigate, they looked up and saw a bright white glowing object moving silently at around twenty-five miles an hour some hundred feet above them.

Dodd and Dale got a good look at it as it passed right over their heads. It was about a hundred feet in diameter, saucer-shaped, with an elongated dome on top that had flashing lights, dark portholes and three large spheres protruding from it. Under the dome was a skirt of brilliant coloured lights that seemed to dance around it. They watched it for about three minutes altogether. As the UFO moved away, it seemed to land in a forest on a nearby hillside.

Shocked and scarcely believing the evidence of their own eyes, Dodd and Dale continued on into town. But before they got there they met another police car coming the other way. The driver stopped. He had seen the huge UFO too. Like all police officers, they were trained observers. Dodd had also been in the RAF before joining the police force and knew a lot about military aircraft.

'The object we saw made no sound at all when it moved,' he said. 'I've never known of any terrestrial craft that can move at any speed without generating some noise.'

However, despite the credibility of the witnesses, there was no official investigation.

5 Men in Black

The Sinister Men

On 30 November 1987, former policeman Philip Spencer had an encounter with a strange 'entity with a green cast' on Ilkley Moor. He also managed to photograph it. Puzzled by what he had seen, he sought out UFO researchers Jenny Randles and Peter Hough, who began investigating the case.

About six weeks later, Spencer was paid an unexpected visit by two men, who introduced themselves as Royal Air Force Intelligence Officers. They flashed ID cards at him and said their names were Davis and Jefferson. They did not beat about the bush; they were there to get the photograph he had taken on Ilkley Moor. The strangers left empty-handed. Spencer no longer had the picture. He had given it to Hough.

It was only after they had gone that Spencer began to wonder how the two strangers had known of the photograph's existence. He had hardly broadcast the fact. As far as he knew, only his wife, Jenny Randles, Peter Hough and another researcher named Arthur Tomlinson had any knowledge of it.

Hough was intrigued too. He contacted RAF Intelligence to find out, but he was told that they had no officers called Davis and Jefferson. What's more, none of their staff had visited Spencer. It was then that Hough realised that Spencer had come up against what American eyewitnesses were already referring to as the 'Men in Black'.

As part of the investigation, clinical psychologist Dr Jim Singleton ran a series of tests on Spencer and confirmed that he was telling the truth 'as he believed it'. And Spencer's experience was far from unique. UFO researchers around the world tell tales of sinister Men in Black, who call on witnesses seemingly with the intention of stealing any physical evidence they might have of the encounter or terrorising them into silence. This sinister cover-up is now so familiar that the perpetrators are known simply as MIBs and they have even had a Hollywood movie made glamorising their activities.

The MIBs first made an appearance in 1947, when a mysterious black-clad stranger turned up in a black Buick sedan car at the home of Harold Dahl, the morning after the Maury Island encounter. The MIB knew what had happened the previous day and invited Dahl out for breakfast. He warned Dahl that he had best keep quiet about what he had seen. 'Silence is the best thing for you and your family,' he said. Dahl was naturally intimidated.

In 1953 when Albert Bender, the founder of the Connecticut-based International Flying Saucer Bureau, was investigating the case again he was visited by three MIBs. They told him to stop his research and threatened his family. He closed down the IFSB just eighteen months after it started. He did, however, make a drawing of one of the men who had visited him and circulated it in the UFO community.

Albert K. Bender's sketch of one of the three Men in Black who visited his Connecticut home in September 1953 and told him to stop investigating UFO mysteries.

Then in 1988, after Amaury Rivera was abducted by aliens in Puerto Rico, he was visited by three black-suited MIBs in his home in Cabo Rojo. They said they were from the CIA and told him to hand over the photographs he had taken. But Rivera had hidden them and, again, they went away empty-handed.

In May 1964, firefighter James Templeton took a photograph of his daughter at a remote marsh near Carlisle, Cumbria. When the film was developed, it showed a man in a silver spacesuit floating in mid-air behind the little girls. Soon after, two men in black suits turned up at the Templeton home in a black Jaguar car.

'They were very strange,' said Templeton, 'asking peculiar questions about the weather and the behaviour of animals.'

They claimed to be from the government but never referred to each other by name, just by numbers. Templeton drove them out to the marsh where the photograph had been taken, but they grew angry when he said he had not seen anyone there that day; he only saw the space-suited man in the photograph after it had been developed.

'They drove away, stranding me alone to walk five miles home,' Templeton said. 'I never heard from them again.'

Who are the MIBs?

Although accounts vary widely, MIBs usually turn up unannounced shortly after a UFO sighting or an encounter with an extraterrestrial. They usually appear in pairs or groups of three. They are dressed in black military uniform with no insignia or in plain black suits, which are always immaculately pressed, white shirt and black hats. And they often arrive in an old-fashioned

Man in Black and triangular UFO (computer generated image).

black car that is in mint condition. Most MIBs produce ID cards and claim to come from a government deparment, a military intelligence agency or a UFO research group. But when their names are checked out, the organisation they say they work for denies all knowledge of them.

MIBs also have an uncannily detailed knowledge of the case, even when the details have not been publicised, and they warn that terrible consequences will ensue if witnesses talk to anyone about their encounter. What makes this all the more unsettling is that they also have detailed information of the victim, often relating things about the victim or the incident that only they could verify. Because the visit often takes place within hours of the UFO incident, victims are left wondering how they acquired this knowledge so quickly.

It stands to reason that the only people with instant access to this kind of information are government intelligence agencies. It is plain that they also have the access to phone calls, faxes and e-mails that would give them the most thorough-going details of any case right away. This would also explain why the organisations they purport to come from deny all knowledge of them. This is standard practice in the intelligence community. The CIA and MI5 will never confirm or deny that any particular individual is working or even has worked for them.

UFOlogists believe that these shadowy strangers are involved in a campaign of disinformation to conceal the true nature of covert government operations, possibly top-secret military programmes, or they could be part of a government-organised conspiracy to prevent the truth about UFO and alien encounters becoming public knowledge.

Are MIBs Aliens?

The phenomenon of 'Men in Black' took an even more sinister twist after the alien abduction of two men at the height of UFO activity in the Maine in October 1975. Nearly a year later, on 11 September 1976, Dr Herbert Hopkins, a psychiatrist who was investigating the abductions, was working alone at home when he got a telephone call from man who said he was UFO researcher. The stranger said he was interested in the case the doctor was investigating and asked if he might visit. Hopkins agreed. But he did not expect that, less than a minute after he had put the phone down, the stranger would appear at the back door.

'I saw no car,' said Hopkins, 'and even if he did have a car, he could not have possibly gotten to my house that quickly from any pay phone.' This was before the days that everyone had a mobile phone.

The strange visitor advised Dr Hopkins to destroy all his records on the abduction case. Then when the conversation turned to the general topic of UFOs, the visitor's speech began to falter. The stranger stood up shakily and stumbled towards the door.

'I must go now,' he said, excusing himself. 'My energy is running low.'

Once the stranger had left, Dr Hopkins began to realise that there was something very odd about his visitor's appearance. Although he wore an old-fashioned black suit, it looked brand new. He had no eyebrows or eyelashes and was completely bald. His skin was strangely wan and he appeared to be wearing lipstick. Some have suggested he was an extraterrestrial in disguise.

MIBs, All in the Mind?

Some MIB encounters have a distinctly surreal feel to them, not unlike the dream-like – or nightmare-like – quality of some alien abduction stories. And it has been suggested by those who are convinced that MIBs are extraterrestrials that the two phenomena are in some way related.

Others have looked for a psychological explanation of the MIB phenomenon. American UFO researcher Dr Alvin Lawson has drawn attention to the fact that the alien figures seen in alien encounters and the strange 'foreign-looking' MIBs both correspond to the archetypes that psychologist Carl Jung discovered lying buried in everyone's unconscious. Lawson believes that something triggers the victim's imagination to draw upon this well of imagery.

'I myself feel certain that accounts given by witnesses reflect what their senses have reported – that, is they do actually perceive humanoids,' he says.

After all, MIBs have been around for some time. Thomas Jefferson, the man who wrote the Declaration of Independence and went on to become the third President of the United States, is said to have received the first idea for the Great Seal of the United States from a mysterious Man in Black who turned up at his home in Virginia. And in his book *The Mothman Prophecies*, veteran UFOlogist John Keel says that Julius Caesar, Napoleon Bonaparte and Malcolm X, among others, were all visited by MIBs – who could well have been aliens.

Running counter to this argument is the fact that government bodies and intelligence agencies are slowly admitting that they have been investigating UFO sightings. Although they still deny that they employ 'Men in Black', some government agencies, including Britain's Ministry of Defence, admit that they have sent out officers to interview witnesses – though they do not say whether they wear black suits or not.

UFOlogist Peter Hough has investigated a number of MIB cases. 'My feelings are that, in some cases, we are dealing with undercover agents, possibly from the Ministry of Defence,' he says. 'But the overwhelming number of MIB cases seem to tie in with UFO phenomena. To my mind, the likeliest possible explanation is that MIBs are intruders from another dimension who have somehow found a way of manifesting in ours. But the whole thing seems to be a charade. There are often comical features about them and they frequently ask trivial questions that have nothing to do with UFOs. The most sinister thing is that they appear to know what's in our minds and then play up to it.'

The Men from the Ministry

Peter Hough's colleague, British UFOlogist Jenny Randles, has unearthed information that the 'Men in Black' are indeed government investigators. The new evidence comes from a small story that broke in the UK's national press on 3 March 1966. It concerned the close encounter of twenty-eight-year-old PC Colin Perks in the

English town of Wilmslow, Cheshire. The story made no great waves among the population generally, but UFOlogists recognised that it was a very impressive case – an unidentified craft had been seen at close quarters by a reliable witness.

PC Perks had his encounter with a UFO at 4:10 a.m. on 7 January 1966.

'It was about the length of a bus and an estimated twenty feet wide,' he said. 'It was elliptical in shape and emanated a greenish-grey glow which I can only describe as an eerie colour.'

It made a mechanical humming noise, but was stationary for about five seconds before it shot off at incredible speed 'in an east-south-easterly direction'. Very quickly, it disappeared from view.

Being a police officer, Perks made his sighting report by the book. He phoned air traffic control at nearby Manchester Airport, gave the information to the staff of the radio telescope at Jodrell Bank and sent a report to his superintendent. The police report then got passed up the chain of command. Eventually it reached the desk of the Deputy Chief Constable of Cheshire, who decided to endorse it, and on 12 January 1966 he sent it to the Ministry of Aviation, part of the Ministry of Defence. As the report was for-warded to them from such a high-ranking official, the MoD was forced to take the matter seriously. They investigated PC Colin Perks and his encounter, and compiled an impressive twenty-page report. A brief mention did surface in the press nearly two months after the original sighting, but then the Perks case disappeared into the files. It languished there for three decades. But in early 1997, under the thirty-year rule, the report was sent to the Public Record Office at Kew, along with hundreds of other UFO reports sent to the Ministry in 1966.

However, the file on the PC Perks case contained a major sur-prise – documented proof that the British government maintained a covert UFO investigation unit, though they had long denied it. Agents from that unit had been directly involved in the Perks case. Here at last was documentary evidence of the 'Men in Black'.

On 13 January 1996, PC Perks' sighting report arrived on the desk of the deputy controller of aircraft research at the Ministry of

Aviation. The following day he forwarded it to the UFO desk, then designated S4f, at the MoD. In doing so, he noted that 'the controller of aircraft in this ministry has seen the reports and considers that some experts should speak to the constable'. So far, so good.

On 18 February 1966, a report classified as 'restricted' about Perks' encounter was sent to S4f by a Flight Lieutenant J.P.H. Mercer of DI (Defence Intelligence) Unit 61e (Air). But the distribution codes on the document show that it was also forwarded to another department. This was DSTI Tech Int (Air). DSTI is the Directorate of Scientific Technical Intelligence – the overall intelligence division of which DI 61e was a part.

In the report Mercer says that someone from DI 61e (Air) went to Wilmslow on 1 February and interviewed PC Perks. The file also includes the plans of a dome-shaped craft drawn up by Perks. The agent also visited the site of his encounter and made a search of the area. During the course of the investigation, DI 61e discovered that a 'glass like substance was found on the adjacent car park... on the morning of the sighting'. But Mercer said he did not think this was unusual. His unit had not connected it with the sighting, nor had they bothered to send it for analysis. Checks with radar stations had not uncovered any unidentified contacts in the area that coincided with Perks' sighting. However, other people in the area also saw a UFO that night. One report came from a Wilmslow woman who had returned home from a dance at around 4 a.m. on the night of 7 January. She reported seeing a green object streak across the sky, in clear view from her bedroom window. S4f also passed her sighting report on to DI 61e (Air).

What is important about the Perks' case is that the British government had always vehemently denied that there was any special intelligence unit that investigated UFO sightings beyond the S4f desk at the Air Ministry. The Mercer document proved there was – DI 61e (Air) – and a forty-five-year-old government cover-up had finally been uncovered.

History of a Cover-up

British government interest in UFOs dates from July 1952, when

Prime Minister Winston Churchill wrote to his Air Minister, Lord Cherwell, asking him to look into the reality of UFO activity in the wake of the wave of reports of flying saucers being seen over Washington. In due course, an official report was prepared that concluded that most UFOs reports were a case of mistaken identity and flying saucers were 'no perceived defence threat'.

Events conspired to contradict this official position almost straight away when a NATO exercise called Operation Mainbrace, underway from 19 to 21 September, was infiltrated in daylight by UFOs. RAF planes chased other anomalous objects over North Yorkshire, and a US aircraft carrier in the North Sea was 'buzzed' by a flying saucer. Under the circumstances, the British authorities were forced to reconsider. On 13 January 1953, a memo bearing the code FC/S.45485/Signals was sent to all RAF station chiefs informing them that there was a new policy on UFOs. This was spelt out in a restricted document dated 16 December. The memo ordered senior staff to report all UFO sightings to the Air Ministry.

'All reports are to be classified "restricted", and personnel are to be warned that they are not to communicate to anyone other than official persons any information about phenomena they have observed,' it said.

This was clear evidence of a flying saucer cover-up. Classification meant that UFO sighting reports were now to fall under the aegis of the Official Secrets Act and people were warned not to talk. At the same time, 'sympathetic' journalists were employed both in the UK and US throughout the 1950s and 1960s to ridicule UFO witnesses and generally debunk the idea that aliens were visiting Earth.

When asked about UFOs, the MoD has replied with a form letter. It reads: 'The Ministry of Defence has no full-time organisation investigating or studying UFOs. Its interest in UFOs is limited to the defence aspects and the department does not undertake to pursue its research, other than for defence implications, to a point where positive correlation with a known object is established.'

After the Perks' file became public the letter was amended, adding that 'secretarial support staff receive sightings via airports, coastguard stations and RAF commands, but do so only as a minor part of their routine work'. This is a tacit admission that there are people working on UFO sightings. But the 'Men in Black' who visited Perks, Spencer and others were not 'secretarial support staff'. Nor are they the medium-grade clerical staff at Air Staff 2A – the current designation of the so-called UFO desk that files sighting reports, speaks to the media and reassures the public that UFOs are being taken seriously by the MoD. Air Staff 2A does no real research, and it never sends people to visit witnesses. Its staff have limited security clearance, so could not read highly classified UFO reports anyway. AS 2A is merely a shop-window. The real work takes place at the back of the store. This is where you find the science and technical staff of the DSTI and defence intelligence units such as DI 55/DI 61e (Air). The Perks case proves that agents from these units do visit UFO witnesses. Some say that these mysterious Men in Black flourishing MoD credentials are sometimes responsible for more intimidating visits. They confiscate physical evidence and cajole witnesses into silence. Since Perks was visited by a DI 61e (Air) agent on 1 February 1966, he has said nothing more about his sighting.

6 The UFOlogists

Stanton Friedman

Nuclear physicist Stanton Friedman is one of America's leading UFOlogists and has been researching the subject for over forty years, ever since a one-dollar book he bought in 1959 sparked his interest. He co-wrote *Crash at Corona* – the definitive study of the Roswell incident –with Don Berliner. In *TOP SECRET/MAJIC*, he investigated the Majestic-12 documents and US government efforts to conceal evidence of alien spacecraft from the American people. He has lectured around the world. He says that he silenced all but a handful of sceptics who refuse to believe that the Earth is being visited by intelligently controlled extraterrestrial spacecraft.

Curiously, Friedman has never seen a flying saucer himself. Instead he is a critical judge of other people's reports. Nevertheless, he says that seeing UFOs is much more common than most people imagine. At his lectures, he asks people whether they have seen a flying saucer. The hands go up reluctantly, he says, 'but they know I'm not going to laugh'. Typically, ten per cent of the audience admit to seeing a UFO. Then he asks how many of them reported it.

'I'm lucky if it's ten per cent of the ten per cent,' says Friedman. 'Sightings of flying saucers are common, reports are not.'

Friedman became interested in the world of UFOs by accident when he was twenty-four. He was ordering books by mail and needed to buy one more to avoid paying shipping charges. The one he chose was *The Report On Unidentified Flying Objects* by Air Force Captain Edward Ruppelt, former director of Project Blue Book. Friedman read the book and was intrigued. He figured that Ruppelt had to know what he was talking about. So he read fifteen more books on UFOs and spent a couple of years digging up as much information as he could.

His conclusion was that there was overwhelming evidence that Earth is being visited by intelligently controlled extraterrestrial spacecraft. However, he believed that, while some flying saucers are alien space ships, most are not. He believes that since July 1947, when two crashed saucers were recovered in New Mexico along with alien bodies, the government has back-engineered spacecraft of its own. Only a few insiders know that this has been done and he calls the cover-up the 'Cosmic Watergate'.

He began investigating the Roswell incident in 1978 after being put in touch with one of the witnesses. He has now interviewed over two hundred witnesses – of those some thirty were involved with the discovery and recovery of the alien craft and the subsequent cover-up of the two crashes. On top of that he has news cuttings from Chicago to the West Coast newspapers on 8 July 1947 and FBI memos that back the story. He also believes that these show that there was a second UFO crash in New Mexico in 1947, 150 miles to the west of Corona, the first crash site, in the plains around San Augustin. He has found eyewitnesses who saw 'a large metallic object' stuck in the ground there.

He is not convinced by Ray Santilli's alien autopsy film though, seeing nothing in it that was associated with a crashed saucer at Roswell or anywhere else. He is also concerned that Santilli has refused to have the film verified. Nor has he released details of the cameraman so that they can be checked out. Friedman likes to look at the evidence.

Friedman is not flattered by being called a UFOlogist. He says that it is supposed to mean a person who has studied the science of UFOlogy, but there are no standards.

'Anybody who reads two books and carries a briefcase thinks he qualifies,' he says.

A big part of the problem of proving that flying saucers really exist is that people make wild claims that cannot be substantiated by the evidence. But he is more annoyed at the failure of the media to do their job. They have failed to dig into what Friedman considers to be the biggest story of the millennium. He believes that the media pay too much attention to what he calls the 'noisy negativists', none of whose arguments stand up under careful scrutiny, he says. 'They sound good, until you look at the evidence and they collapse of their own weight.'

He points out that there have been five large-scale scientific studies on UFOs, ten doctoral theses have been published and hundreds of papers have been produced by scientists. But most people, especially the debunkers, seem to be totally ignorant of this enormous amount of information. In his lectures he goes through the five scientific studies and asks how many people have read them. Less than two per cent of these people, who are plainly interested in the topic, are familiar with even one of the studies.

Friedman is also invited to speak to government bodies and gets a good response. But he finds that the question-and-answer sessions with the government people are a one-way street. They ask him a lot of questions but they do not reveal anything. He has spoken at Los Alamos National Laboratory and pulled a huge crowd. He has also given testimony to Congressional hearings in 1968 and at the United Nations in 1978.

Friedman finds being trained as a scientist is very useful in his work as a UFOlogist. It has meant that his approach is objective, painstaking, honest and scientific. Much of what he worked on as a scientist was classified. He wrote classified documents and had a security clearance. This gave him the opportunity to find out how security works and was good training for searching government archives for classified material later. Now he now lives in Canada and works on less sensitive science research projects such as pollution control and food irradiation.

He believes that the Majestic-12 documents prove President Harry Truman set up a super-secret group of top people from the fields of science, the military and intelligence to learn about alien spacecraft. He has spent over twelve years trawling through fifteen government archives, checking out whether these documents are real. Repeatedly, he has found confirmation of details in the documents that no one but insiders could have known. Friedman has even collected $1,000 from one critic who claimed one of the typefaces used in one of the MJ-12 documents was wrong.

'It was an absurd challenge, since I'd spent weeks searching through the government archives and he hadn't,' says Friedman. 'It also typifies the intellectual bankruptcy of the pseudo-science of anti-

UFOlogy. I've yet to see a good anti MJ-12 argument.'

Friedman has had no chance to check out the data on alien abductions, but believes that every abduction story should be taken on its own merits. He has faith in abduction researchers because of his dealings with them and thinks that some people have been abducted.

According to Friedman's theory the government used five major arguments for withholding evidence from the public. The first is that it wants to figure out how flying saucers work because they make wonderful weapons delivery and defence systems. Secondly, it needs to do this before any potential enemy does. Thirdly, if this information was released, the younger generation would see humankind merely as 'earthlings' – which is what we are from an alien point of view. Friedman thinks this would be a great benefit. The problem with that is that there is no government on earth that wants its citizens to owe their primary allegiance to the planet rather than their country. Fourthly, there are certain religious fundamentalists who maintain humankind is the only intelligent life in the universe – that means that UFOs must be the work of the devil. These fundamentalists have huge political influence and their religions would be destroyed if they were proved wrong. Finally, any announcement that the aliens were here would cause widespread panic. Some people would believe that were aliens are here to slaughter us. Others would reason that the aliens were obviously more technologically advanced than us and would bring with them new energy sources, new transportation systems, new computers and new communication systems. As a result the stock market would crash and there would be untold economic consequences.

However, Friedman still believes that the public is ready to hear the truth about UFOs. There would, of course, be some people who did not want to know – just as there are five per cent of the American public who do not believe that man has been to the moon. But the evidence about UFOs could be presented honestly and openly.

'I certainly don't think we should put technical data about flying saucers out on the table,' he says. 'But our planet is being visited by intelligent aliens. It's time we grew up.'

Jaques Vallee

Steven Spielberg's movie *Close Encounters of the Third Kind* made Jacques Vallee the most famous UFOlogist in the world. The François Truffaut character is based on the French researcher. Although he became a computer scientist for the Department of Defense, Vallee began his career as an astrophysicist. As a young man, it was curiosity that led him to study astronomy, but that same curiosity led him on into the world of UFOs. He does not find studying anomalous phenomena unscientific, pointing out that Nobel prize winner Niels Bohr said that all science starts with an anomaly.

He was working at the Paris Observatory when he first got interest in UFOs. They had observed a number of 'unidentified satellites'. However, when the scientists there were ordered to destroy the data concerning these 'anomalies' instead of sending it to their colleagues for further study, he rebelled.

This was during the early 1960s when the idea that UFOs were connected to alien intervention was widespread. Back then, he found that the 'extraterrestrial hypothesis' seemed to match witnesses' accounts. But since then, thousands more cases have been reported and statistical models could be used to analyse them. This has forced Vallee to take another, more critical look at the extraterrestrial hypothesis.

Vallee already had a passion for religious history, myths, occultism and parapsychology and, around 1968, he realised that many aspects of the UFO phenomenon were also present in the folklore of every culture. By 1975, he got the idea of combining these disciplines by considering the UFO phenomenon, not as simply a manifestation of extraterrestrial visitors, but as a control system that had been in existence since the beginning of humankind. He points out that UFO sightings did not start with Kenneth Arnold in 1947. Elements of the phenomena existed before. He believes that the wheels of Ezekiel, cherubim and burning bushes seen in biblical times, the flying goblins in luminous chariots of the Middle Ages, the phantom airships of the nineteenth century, the 'ghost rockets' of 1946 and the extraterrestrial spacecraft seen today are all essentially the same phenomenon.

As we learn more about the history and geographical distribution of the phenomenon, the standard extraterrestrial hypothesis leads to glaring contradictions, Vallee says. He believes that objects and beings connected to the UFO phenomenon are symbolic, or even theatrical, manifestations, rather than a systematic alien exploration where abductions are conducted for the purposes of so-called 'biological studies', as other UFOlogists suggest.

'We are also looking at some form of non-human consciousness,' he says. 'However, one must be wary of concluding that we are dealing with an "extraterrestrial race".'

Vallee aims to shatter the assumption that 'UFO' means 'extraterrestrial spacecraft'. He believes that behind these enigmatic luminous phenomena is a form of intelligence capable of manipulating space-time and influencing human evolution. In his best-selling book *Confrontations*, published in 1990, he analysed over a hundred UFO encounters using scientific methods, and concludes that the aliens visiting us come from another dimension.

Vallee is the champion of a bold new speculative physics. He believes that objects capable of gradually appearing and disappearing on the spot are modifying space-time topology. This validates the multidimensional models of the universe that theoretical physicists have been working on in recent years.

But he does not totally reject the extraterrestrial hypothesis, just the hard-nosed American approach to it. He believes that we share our existence with other forms of consciousness that influence the topology of our environment and affect the human mind psychically. Vallee has been accused of contradicting himself, because at times he emphasises the physical and material aspects of UFOs, while at others stressing the psychic and paranormal side. But this contradiction is in the data, he says.

Vallee is a believer in alien abduction, but believes that hypnotising abductees as practised in America is unethical, unscientific and perhaps even dangerous. He has investigated over seventy abduction cases. From his interviews with witnesses he has no doubt that the large majority of abductees have had a close encounter with an object emitting electromagnetic radiation, pulsed at hyper-frequencies. The effects on the human brain of these are unknown, so hypnotising the victims could put them at risk. He points out that UFO encounters are dangerous enough to humans as it is, with large amounts of energy confined to a restricted space.

One of the abduction cases Vallee studied was that of Franck Fontaine, who was abducted on 26 November 1979 from the Parisian suburb of Cergy-Pontoise after seeing a bright light in the sky. Vallee was particularly interested in the case because he was born in Pontoise and went to the same school as Fontaine. Although Fontaine admitted, two years later, that the abduction was a hoax, Vallee does not believe the explanations that have been given. They do not correspond to his knowledge of the area or the psychological state of the witnesses.

'I don't believe it was a UFO, but I do think that Franck was actually abducted,' he says. 'Someone is hiding something.'

The dozen or so 'implants' he has examined have not been mysterious in nature. Analysis showed that many of them were the tips of rusty needles, fragments of insects or other natural material embedded in the flesh. However, Vallee was the first to draw attention to the subject of animal mutilations over twenty years ago in his book *La Grande Manipulation* ('The Great Manipulation'), but he has not published research because he was unable to prove the link between the mutilations and the UFO phenomenon. He does believe that the link exists, though.

Vallee finds the USAF's latest explanation of the Roswell incident – that it was the crash of a balloon carrying a basket full of mannequins – laughable.

'The most recent report from the Air Force is even more absurd than all the other "explanations" given previously,' he says. 'The fact that an extremely strange object came down near Roswell and that the military made every effort to discourage research into the incident and continues to do so is beyond doubt. However, this doesn't mean that the object in question was a UFO.'

For Vallee, the jury is still out on the Roswell incident. He believes that the idea of a crash is only plausible if you believe it to be a deliberate demonstration on the part of an external intelligence. In the meantime he is investigating nineteen other different crash cases.

Vallee believes that every country's armed forces uses the UFO phenomenon to cover up operations involving advanced or illegal weapons. This started in the USSR as early as 1967, when the KGB spread rumours about UFOs in a region where the inhabitants had seen rockets being launched that were carrying satellites in violation of international agreements. UFO rumours also cloak remotely controlled rigid airships that the military use to gather electromagnetic data. An American soldier he knows approached one of these craft standing in a clearing in Germany during manoeuvres before the Gulf War and he has read US patent applications describing them.

Generally Vallee's scientific colleagues are open-minded about UFOs. They have no time for grandiose conspiracy theories, but they do admit the existence of a 'non-standard phenomenon'. During his forty years of UFO investigations, he has discovered that the UFO phenomenon is considerably more complex than he used to think. It cannot be explained simply by an extrapolation of current human technology.

'We are faced with a phenomenon that underlies the whole of human history, manipulates the real world and seems to obey laws that bear no relationship to those we hitherto imagined,' he says. 'I believe we're entering a particularly exciting period in the phenomenon's history, since we now have the opportunity of re-examining all the various hypotheses.'

More recently, Vallee has published a memoir of his years in UFOlogy called *Science Interdite* ('Forbidden Science'). This also examines the validity of the US Army's secret 'Memorandum Pentacle'.

Bob Lazar

Soft-spoken physicist Bob Lazar is one of the most controversial figures in UFOlogy. A man with a strong scientific background, he has been involved in the 'back-engineering' of alien spacecraft at the notorious Area 51 in the Nevada desert.

In 1982 he was a member of a scientific team at the US military's Groom Dry Lake installation. There he worked on a top-secret project to unravel the technology used by alien spacecraft that had been recovered from various crashes. Nine disc-shaped craft were held under armed guard in an underground section of the base known as 'S4'. The job of Lazar's team was to find out what made these flying saucers tick and whether their components could be replicated with materials found on Earth.

Many people have poured scorn on Lazar's story since it was first aired in a TV interview in 1989. As a child he was eccentric. His resumé includes bankruptcy and an association with a Las Vegas brothel. Lazar is easily discredited. Officials at Area 51 deny that anyone named Robert Lazar ever worked there – just as they once denied that Area 51 itself existed. But a salary statement issued by the United States Department of Naval Intelligence proves that Lazar did work in Area 51 for the five months as he claimed.

And when it comes to engineering, it is plain that Lazar knows what he is talking about. He has an impressive list of technical qualifications and is a scientist with a pedigree. In the early 1980s he was employed on several projects at the Los Alamos National Laboratory, New Mexico, where the first atomic bomb was developed. At Los Alamos, he conducted experiments with proton-scattering equipment and worked with high-energy particle accelerators. The work he did there was on the cutting edge of the new physics and could open the way to faster-than-light travel. As a prominent member of the town's scientific community, he earned himself an appearance on the front page of the *Los Alamos Monitor* when he installed a jet engine in a Honda CRX.

Despite the efforts made to paint him as slightly cracked, Lazar's account of what went on in Area 51 is lucid and concise, clearly not the ramblings of a disturbed mind. With his scientific background, his observations have a solid foundation. His specific task at Area 51 was to investigate the propulsion system of a small flying saucer dubbed 'the sports model', which was kept in one of the S4 hangars built into the side of a mountain. He witnessed a brief, low altitude test flight of the disc.

The sports model was some forty feet in diameter and fifteen feet high. It had three levels. The top level was an observation deck nine feet across, with portholes. Below that were the control consoles and seats, which were too small and too near the floor for adult humans to use comfortably. The main cabin had a headroom of just six feet. Also in the central level was an antimatter reactor and, located directly below it on the lower level, were the three 'gravity amplifiers', connected to the reactor by wave guides. He worked on this propulsion system both in situ in the craft and on the bench in the lab.

The power source for the sports model and the eight other discs in S4 was an 'antimatter reactor', Lazar says. These reactors were fuelled by an orange-coloured, super-heavy material called 'Element 115'. This mysterious element was the source of the 'Gravity A' wave as yet undiscovered by terrestrial science. It also provided the antimatter radiation required to power the saucer in interstellar flight.

The flying saucers in S4 have two modes of travel. For local travel, near the surface of a planet, they use their gravity generators to balance the planet's gravitational field and ride a Gravity A wave like a cork on the ocean. During interstellar travel, covering distances that would take aeons even travelling at close to the speed of light, the Gravity A wave from the nucleus of Element 115 is amplified. This bends space and time in the same way it is bent in the intense gravitational field generated by a black hole. As the saucer travels through space, time is 'bent' around the craft. By distorting space and time in this manner, the disc can travel across vast expanses of space at incredible speeds. This is the same principle used by the *Enterprise*'s 'warp drive' in *Star Trek*.

Terrestrial rockets push the craft towards their destination by blasting jets of hot gas in the opposite direct, while alien craft 'pull' the destination towards them. Lazar explains how this works with the analogy of a rubber sheet with a stone, representing the spacecraft, on it. To go to any particular destination, you pinch the rubber sheet at that point and pull it towards the stone. Then, when you let got, the rubber sheet springs back, pulling the stone – or space-craft-with it.

'In a spacecraft that can exert a tremendous gravitational field by itself,' he says, 'you could sit in any particular place, turn on the gravity generator, and actually warp space and time and "fold" it. By shutting that off, you'd click back and you'd be at a tremendous distance from where you started.'

Although this type of propulsion appears to be the stuff of sci-ence fiction, many scientists believe that faster-than-light travel may be possible. Cambridge University's Lucasian professor of mathematics Stephen Hawking has suggested that interstellar trav-el might be achievable via natural or manmade 'worm-holes' in the fabric of space-time. Understanding how this works in practice is a bit more taxing, of course.

Inside the flying saucers' antimatter reactor, Lazar says, Element 115 is transmuted into another esoteric material called 'Element 116'. This is highly unstable and decays, releasing antimatter. The antimatter then reacts with matter inside the reactor in a total anni-hilation reaction, where one hundred per cent of the matter–anti-matter is converted into energy. This energy is used to amplify the Gravity A wave given off the Element 115 and the heat generated by reaction is converted to electricity via a solid state thermo-elec-tric generator.

The alien craft were saucer-shaped to diffuse the electrical charges generated by the antimatter reactor. In flight, Lazar says, the bottom of the alien craft glowed blue and began to hiss like a high voltage charge does on a sphere.

'It's my impression that the reason that they're round and have no sharp edges is to contain the high voltage,' says Lazar. 'If you've seen a high voltage change system's insulators, things are round or else you get a corona discharge.'

The craft's high voltage makes them hiss when they take off. Otherwise they are silent. And the hissing stops when they have climbed to twenty or thirty feet. 'There are just too many things that Lazar knew about the discs that can't be explained in any other way,' said George Knapp, the TV journalist who first interviewed him.

Lazar says that, at one time, there were Soviet scientists and mathematicians working at Area 51, alongside the Americans there. He did not know whether they were actually allowed to work on the alien craft, but believes that they were employed on the scientific and mathematical theory that underpinned his group's practical work.

They were kicked out after a major breakthrough had been made in understanding how the discs and their propulsion systems worked. They were none too happy about this. Lazar says that in the aftermath of their exclusion, paranoia at the base soared. Employees were issued with firearms, in case the Soviets tried to kidnap them.

During his time at Area 51, Lazar had to read a document the size of a telephone directory, which revealed that the top-secret base at Groom Lake was not the only US government facility back-engineering ET technology. The US government's admission that other secret bases do exist lent weight to Lazar's story. However, what goes on in them is still beyond top secret. Since Lazar's Area 51 security clearance was mysteriously revoked at the end of the 1980s, he has been subjected of intense harassment. His house and car have been broken into and he has been shot at by unseen snipers in an attempt to discourage him from divulging the secrets of S4.

Edgar Fouche

Like Bob Lazar, Edgar Fouche worked at Area 51 and has since spent his time telling the world about what is going on there. Fouche is a true insider who spent twenty-eight years with the US Air Force and Department of Defense. During that time, he was stationed at top-secret sites, including the nuclear test site in Nevada, the Nellis Test Range and the Groom Lake Air Base, home of Area 51. Fouche's work in intelligence, electronics, communications and a number of black programmes has given him inside information on some of America's most classified technological developments, including the super-secret SR-71 and SR-75 spy planes and the TR-3B, which many people believe is sometimes mistake for the 'Flying Triangle'.

However, during the 1980s when President Reagan was in power, he became completely disenchanted with the defence industry. It was full of fraud and abuse of power and he decided that he could not be associated with it anymore. He was suffering serious medical problems at the time and did not think he was going to live much longer. So he decided to speak up.

In this, he was helped by five friends who served with him in Vietnam. One was a former SR-71 spy plane pilot. Two of them went on to work for the National Security Agency. A fourth friend's father had worked for the NSA for twenty years and the fifth worked for the Department of Defense. He also gleaned information about the TR-3B by talking to pilots.

His buddy who was the SR-71 pilot told him that once, when he was flying back across the South China Sea, he saw a shadow fall across the cockpit. The aircraft started to nose down and the avionics went crazy. When he looked up to find out what was happening, he saw a UFO that was so big it completely blocked out the sun. It was oval and surrounded by a shimmering energy field, and he reckoned that it was three hundred feet across.

What really amazed Fouche was that all the pilots he spoke to reported encounters with UFOs. Some had seen circular UFOs, others had encountered plasma balls that seemed to dance around the craft. These reports were all the more impressive because the SR-71 can fly at over 60,000 feet. This gives it enormous visibility. If something is up there, an SR-71 is going to see it.

Fouche's contacts told him that the development of the TR-3B started in 1982 as part of a top-secret project named 'Aurora', whose aim was to build and test advanced aerospace vehicles. He discovered that around 35 per cent of the US government's 'Star Wars' budget had been siphoned off to finance it. The TR-3B is a triangular nuclear-powered aerospace platform and is undoubtedly the most exotic aerospace programme in existence. The designation 'TR' stands for tactical reconnaissance. This means the craft is designed to get to the target and stay there long enough pick up information on the enemy's deployment and send it back. The advantage of being powered by a nuclear reactor is that it can stay aloft for a long time without refuelling.

Its advanced propulsion system also allows it to hover silently for long periods. The circular crew compartment is located at the centre of TR-3B's triangular airframe. It is surrounded by a plasma-filled accelerator ring, called the Magnetic Field Disrupter, which generates a magnetic vortex and neutralises the pull of gravity. The MFD does not actually power the craft; what it does is effectively reduce its mass. Propulsion is achieved by three multimode gas-propelled thrusters mounted on each corner of the triangle. But MFD makes the aircraft incredibly light. It can fly at Mach 9 speeds vertically and horizontally, and can outmanoeuvre anything except UFOs.

One of Fouche's sources who worked on the TR-3B told him that they were working on the possibility of developing the MFD technology so that it not only reduces mass but also creates a force that repels gravity. This would give the TR-3B a propulsion system that would allow it to routinely fly to the Moon or Mars. This anti-gravity system is how UFOs work and Fouche is convinced that the TR-3B has been developed through the back-engineering of alien technology.

Fouche believes that the black triangles tracked by the Belgian Air Force in the late 1980s and early 1990s were TR-3Bs. He has a simple rule: if it is triangular it is terrestrial, if it is circular or tubular it is extraterrestrial. He says that the US government could easily get round treaty agreements that prohibit testing advanced aircraft over Europe. These agreements, he points out, say that they cannot fly an aircraft over a friendly country without that country being informed. It would be easy enough to inform the Belgian government on the sly. After all, the US is not supposed to have nuclear weapons in the UK or Japan, but they do.

Groom Lake's six-mile-long runway is the longest in the world. Fouche says that it was built to accommodate the CIA's latest super-hi-tech spy plane, the 'Penetrator' or SR-75; 'SR' stands for strategic reconnaissance. It can exceed Mach 7 with speeds of over

28,000 miles an hour at an altitude of 40,000 feet and can reach any point on the Earth within three hours. This plane is so secret that the US government does not even admit to its existence. After the SR-71 Blackbird was retired in 1990, the US Air Force said that it would not be replaced because satellites provided all the military's high-level reconnaissance needs. But Fouche's sources say that the SR-75 has been designed to service spy satellites in orbit. It acts as a 'mothership' and launches unmanned SR-74, or Scramp, craft. Operated by remote control, these can place satellites in space, reaching altitudes of 95 miles and speeds of 6,250 miles an hour, or Mach 15.

Fouche was assigned to Groom Lake in 1979 because he was one of the few people who had the necessary top-secret clearance. He was certified to work with particular equipment which, even years after the event, he was not prepared to discuss. He had been working at Nellis Air Force Base at the time and was told that he was being temporarily reassigned, but was given no idea of where he was going to be sent. Some thirty technicians were herded onto a blue bus with blacked-out windows. There were two guards on board, armed with M16 rifles. They told the passengers not to speak unless spoken to. This is how Fouche ended up at Groom Lake.

The conditions were extremely oppressive. He was issued with heavy glasses, like welders' goggles. These had thick lenses that blocked peripheral vision and prevented the wearer seeing further than thirty metres ahead. Everywhere he went, he was escorted by a soldier carrying an M16 who would never talk to him. He could not even go to the lavatory alone.

According to Fouche, the military used sinister mind-control techniques on employees. One of his five collaborators named Sal was a victim of this. A former NSA electronic intelligence expert, he had helped develop Magnetic Field Disruption. After two-years at a top-secret NSA facility, he came down with what he thought was the flu. He went to see the facility's doctor, who gave him some medication and told him to go home and rest. The next day, Sal had no memory of where he worked or who he worked for.

When his brother contacted the NSA, he was told that Sal's contract had been terminated. Sal's memory has not returned and the only evidence he has that he worked at the NSA facility at all is a few scribbled notes and his pay slips.

Security at Area 51 was so tight that a key card and a code were needed for every door. Fouche is very sceptical about people who claim to have been at Groom Lake and accidentally stumbled into a hangar with a UFO inside. His twenty-eight years with the Department of Defense and the US Air Force taught him that anything that was top-secret was protected by numerous levels of security.

However, in Area 51 there is a facility on the Papoose Lake site called the Defense Advanced Research Center, which extends for ten storeys underground. It was built in the early 1980s with Strategic Defense Initiative money. The DARC is the centre for what is officially designated 'Foreign Artefacts' – this means alien artefacts. Crashed and recovered alien technology is stored there. The DARC is where all the analysis of 'extraterrestrial biological entities' – alien creatures – and back-engineering takes place.

Fouche says that the reason the US government cannot come clean about what they are up to at Area 51 is because, since the birth of the UFO phenomenon in 1947, it has consistently violated people's constitutional rights. The government considers anything that it cannot control a threat, he says. It cannot control the alien agenda, so it tries to control any information surrounding it. People who find out too much about UFOs or aliens either disappear or have been killed, he says. The government would be held accountable if the facts got out and it could not handle that.

David Adair

Another witness to what is going on at Area 51 is space scientist David Adair. He became involved in the world of UFOs through his lifelong passion for science and rocketry.

Adair was a child prodigy. He built his first rocket at the age of eleven. This was no fourth-of-July firework. He fashioned it from sophisticated alloys, using tools and fuels from his father's machine shop.

Then, in 1968, he set out to build a new type of rocket which used powerful electromagnetic fields to contain and harness the thermonuclear energy from a fusion reaction. Although this sounds exotic, it was not his original idea. He got the plans from the long-range planning division of NASA's Marshall Space Flight Center in Huntsville, Alabama. They had come up with the theoretical designs for fifty different types of engine. Only two of them used conventional liquid fuel or solid propellants, so fusion was the obvious the way to go. The one that Adair decided to build was a remarkable design. At the time he wondered why NASA had never made it themselves. Later he realised that they probably chose not to develop it for political reasons. If you developed an efficient fusion-based propulsion system, oil and gas would be redundant. Nevertheless the fourteen-year-old Adair saw the design's potential and, through Republican Congressman John Ashbrook, he got a $1-million grant to build it.

But the grant came with strings attached. The Department of Defense were involved. He was prohibited from telling anyone about what he was building. And for Adair the outside world ceased to exist as he worked on the rocket day and night for the next three years. In 1971, when Adair was seventeen, the rocket was ready to be tested. General Curtis LeMay, the project manager, decided that the rocket was too powerful to be tested outside a secure military facility, so he scheduled a test at White Sands Missile Range in New Mexico.

When Adair was at White Sands preparing for the test, a black DC-9 arrived. It was carrying Dr Arthur Rudolph, one of the designers of the Saturn-5 moon rocket. Originally Rudolph had worked on the Nazi German V-2 programme, but after the war he had been taken to America. Adair told Rudolph that, proportionately, his rocket was a thousand times more powerful than the Saturn-5, and Rudolph was furious.

When Adair was programming his rocket's guidance system, his military bosses gave him a precise location for the landing. The co-ordinates they gave him specified a place four hundred miles away in an area called Groom Lake in Nevada. This puzzled Adair as all the maps showed there was an empty dry lakebed.

After the rocket was launched successfully, Adair was told to get on board the DC-9. They flew him to Groom Lake and, as they came in to land, he could see the huge runways and a huge base that had not appeared on the map. This, he was informed, was Area 51.

When he arrived at Groom Lake, Adair thought he was there to collect his rocket. But he was bundled onto an electric golf cart and driven over to three large hangars. As he got close to the buildings, he could see that they were new, but they had been painted to look much older. The middle hangar was the area of two football fields. Once he was inside, warning lights began flashing, guard rails sprang up and an area of the floor about seven hundred square feet started to descend. Adair realised they were on a huge lift. It went down through solid rock and, when it stopped, Adair found himself the biggest underground space he had ever seen. It contained a lot of aircraft. Most of them were covered up, but he recognised one as the XB-70, an experimental aircraft. It was huge. But he also noticed a number of craft that were a strange teardrop shape with their surfaces perfectly smooth in all directions. The most peculiar thing about them was that they did not have any of the intake or exhaust ports that are needed by jet engines. In fact, they had no visible means of propulsion, yet they were surrounded by support equipment and looked quite capable of flying. Looking back, he now thinks that they used some kind of electromagnetic or flux-field propulsion.

Still in the golf cart, he was driven over to a big set of doors. The driver jumped out and put his hand on a panel. It flashed and the doors opened. We know these things now as optical hand-print scanners, but in 1971 they were the stuff of science fiction. Inside the air was cold and the lighting was strange. There was plenty of light, but nothing seemed to cast a shadow. He was then shown a huge engine that was about the size of a bus. It looked like two octopuses linked together by their tentacles. When Adair examined it, he realised it was some kind of giant version of the motor in his rocket.

His companions explained that this engine used a fusion reaction similar the one he had designed and they wanted his opinion on the firing mechanism. The whole situation struck Adair as bizarre. Why didn't they ask the people who built it, he enquired. He was told they were on leave. So Adair asked to look at their design notes. This seemed to annoy the people who had brought him there.

'Look son, do you want to help your country or not?' they said.

Adair believes that the engine was extraterrestrial in origin. Although it was huge, he could not see a single bolt, rivet or screw holding it together. The surface was perfectly smooth and, although the room was cold, it felt warm to the touch. Whenever he touched the surface, bluish white waves swirled out from his hands and disappeared into the material. They would stop each time he moved his hand away. He climbed up on top of the engine and looked inside. He saw a large container holding bundles of tubes. These were filled with some kind of liquid. Adair's overall impression was that it was organic – part mechanical, part biological. He realised it had been made using non-terrestrial techniques and materials.

He shrugged his shoulders and told his companions that he had no idea how the thing worked. The manufacturing techniques used were very different from anything he had ever seen before. He reasoned that it could not have been built by American engineers or by the Soviets. As it dawned on him that it must have been built using extraterrestrial technology, he got angry. Flying saucers had landed and the government were keeping it a secret. When Adair expressed his outrage at this, his companions shouted at him to get away from the device.

Adair does not think that the engine was working too well, though they have had three decades to work on it since then and he hopes they have been successful. He could certainly see the potential. Adair's own rocket was puny by comparison but it channelled enormous amounts of energy out of the back of the rocket for propulsion. He believes that the alien engine could have managed to contain all the incredible energy generated by the fusion reaction inside the propulsion system, producing a 'field effect' outside the craft. This would create a huge 'gravitation well' which would break through the fabric of space-time. Space would be folded back on itself, allowing the craft to travel vast distances in an instant, without exceeding the speed of light.

However, he is still angry that this device and other exotic craft are in government hands and all their amazing technology is hidden from the rest of the world. Meanwhile people at NASA are struggling to send small spacecraft to Mars. The fact that the US government are withholding knowledge of their contact with other civilisations he also finds incredible.

'These are ET civilisations we could learn so much from,' Adair says. 'When I think of all the ways that we could advance with this knowledge of ET contact, it makes me sick that this information is hidden.'

Since his visit to Area 51 in 1971, Adair has worked as a technology transfer consultant, redesigning space-programme technology for commercial applications. He has an office in Ventura, California. But he has not forgotten what he saw.

On 9 April 1997, Adair testified to a Congressional hearing in Washington, D.C. as part of the campaign for full UFO disclosure. The hearings were organised by the Center for the Study of Extraterrestrial Intelligence and gave key witnesses, including military personnel and pilots, the opportunity to lobby the US government. David Adair was under oath when he told the Congressional panel what he had seen in Area 51 and, unexpectedly, the Congressmen immediately got confirmation that he was telling the truth.

During his testimony, Adair mentioned that the device he had seen was covering in strange markings. He remembered what they looked like and drew them for the panel. Also giving testimony was an attorney from North Carolina named Steven Lovekin, who had top-secret clearance when he worked as a cryptologist at the Pentagon in the 1950s. As military aide, he had given regular briefings to President Eisenhower on UFO activity. In that capacity, he had been shown a piece of metal that he was told came from a downed flying saucer. It was covered in strange markings – the same markings Adair had seen in Area 51.

Wendelle Stevens

Wendelle Stevens' involvement with UFOs began in 1947 when he was assigned to the Air Technical Intelligence Center at Wright Field in Dayton, Ohio, home to the USAF's various in-house UFO study programmes, Sign, Grudge and Blue Book. That year, Stevens was sent from Ohio to Alaska to supervise a squadron of B-29 bombers that were being used to map the arctic. However, he discovered there was a hidden agenda behind their polar mission. The B-29s were equipped with cutting-edge electronic detection technology and cameras to detect and film 'foo fighters' as UFOs were then known.

Stevens's security clearance was not high enough to allow him to see the footage the B-29s had shot before it was sent to Washington, but the pilots told him of their UFO encounters. Many of his pilots saw UFOs soar rapidly into the sky and fly off as the B-29s approached. In most cases, they caused electromagnetic disturbances to the plane's instrumentation, often affecting the engines. On one occasion a UFO approached a B-29 head on. Then, before they collided, it slammed into reverse, manoeuvred itself around next to the wing and stayed there.

Astounded by these revelations, Stevens asked his superiors if he could pursue an investigation into the UFO phenomenon. He was told he could only do so outside of official military channels. So, in 1963, after twenty-three years' active service, he retired and began a new career as a UFO researcher.

He began collecting newspaper clippings of UFOs from all over the world. Where photographs had been printed, he would write to the people who had taken them and ask for a copy. Now he boasts the world's largest collection of UFO photographs – over three thousand images in all – along with a vast library of UFO film and videos.

To establish the authenticity of the photographs, he visits the person who took it and investigates their encounter. He also examines their camera equipment and takes his own photographs from the same spot, so that he can compare relative scale and distances. After these preliminary checks, he subjects the photograph to a series of analytical procedures. Today he uses computer techniques. It was easier in the old days, he says, when all a photographic expert had to do was to make a large-scale blow-up and examine it with a magnifying glass.

Stevens is one of the few UFOlogists who has made a career of studying contactees. In 1976 he was the first researcher to investigate the claims of Swiss contactee Eduard 'Billy' Meier, who was in telepathic contact with aliens and photographed their spaceships coming into land. At Stevens' behest, Meier submitted his evidence for analysis to scientists at McDonnell Douglas, IBM and NASA's Jet Propulsion Laboratory. Their results were inconclusive. However, computer analysis of one of Meier's pictures reveals a model next to a fake tree and models of flying saucers were found in Meier's home. Nonetheless, Stevens believes Meier is genuine.

Stevens decided to specialise in contactees because they presented a unique opportunity to learn about extraterrestrials and their possible agendas. If possible, he sets up a two-way dialogue, asking contactees to pose questions to the extraterrestrials for him next time they meet. Sometimes he gets an answer.

One of the most important contactee cases he investigated was that of Bill Herrmann, who lived in Charleston, South Carolina, near the Air Force base there. He and his wife repeatedly saw a UFO, which flew in a darting motion with sharp, angular turns, unlike the smooth turns of a plane. One night in 1977, when he was trying to get a closer look at it through binoculars, Herrmann was abducted. He was enveloped in a beam of blue light, which drew him up inside the UFO. The extraterrestrials he encountered inside the craft were friendly. They came from one of the twin stars in the Reticulum system. When he asked them questions, he would hear their replies in English inside his head. They told him that the darting movements of their craft were made to avoid any radar lock-on. Radar-guided weapons had previously been responsible for the crashes of three of their ships. They also told Herrmann that they wanted their downed ships back and were prepared to negotiate, but the US government was too hostile to deal with. After this first abduction experience, Herrmann was invited back onto the craft another five times.

When Stevens began investigating the Herrmann case, he discovered that the Reticulans were sending Herrmann vast amounts of information when he was in a trance-like state. He transcribed the transmission in automatic writing. The result was numerous pages of text in a totally unknown alphabet, along with schematic diagrams of their propulsion system. The complex technical information he was provided with was way beyond current human scientific knowledge and Herrmann could never have acquired it from any terrestrial source.

From his work with contactees, Stevens has discovered that there are many different kinds of extraterrestrials. They come from different places and have different languages, morphologies, technologies and agendas. The largest group are the various humanoid species who often tell contactees that they come from the Pleiades star system. The next largest group are the well-known 'Greys', which again comprise a number of different races.

Stevens has also carried out research on Area 51 and tracked down Derek Hennesy, a former security guard who worked on level two of S4, the famous underground complex where Lazar had worked on alien propulsion systems. During his time there, Hennesy saw nine bays for flying saucer bays on level one. There were a further seven bays on level two with three identical alien craft in the first three bays. Hennesy also saw large tubes that contained the preserved bodies of dead Greys. After Stevens first interviewed Hennesy, Hennesy disappeared for a while. When he re-emerged he claimed to have no knowledge of what he had previously seen or said.

However, Stevens had another friend who works as an engineer at Area 51 and says it is engaged in bridging the gap between alien technology and our own. He has built simulators to train human pilots to fly flying saucers. There are two extraterrestrials at Area 51 who can fly alien craft. They have been trying to train humans to do this, but not very successfully. So far they are limited to flights within the atmosphere. They have not yet mastered flight in deep space, but they can hover using some kind of gravity propulsion.

Stevens thinks that there is little chance that the curtain of official secrecy surrounding UFOs will be lifted in the near future. The government have kept what they know a secret for fifty years and he expects them to do so for another fifty. Governments have far too much to lose from any official disclosure, he reckons. The impact on society would be incalculable. The only way the world's governments would admit to the reality of alien visitations is if a group of extraterrestrials makes its presence visible on a massive scale, he says. Stevens believes that there are signs that this may be about to occur in Mexico, where there was an increase in the number of sightings in the 1990s.

Peter Gersten

For twenty years, New York criminal defence attorney Peter Gersten specialised in murder and drug cases. But then, in 1977, as the lawyer for the UFO group Ground Saucer Watch, he took the CIA to court and won. It was a historic victory for UFOlogy.

The suit was filed under the Freedom of Information Act. Ground Saucer Watch were trying to force the CIA to release just five UFO-related documents the agency had in its possession. But Gersten expanded the case. Under the FOIA it was as easy to create a lawsuit to get the CIA to release all the UFO document it had as it was to get just five. As a result, in 1979, the CIA was forced to release nine hundred pages of UFO-related documents – the first time that any US intelligence agency had ever released previously classified UFO information to the public. A further fifty-seven documents were withheld. But the case showed beyond any doubt that the CIA, which had previously denied any involvement in UFOs, had been studying them for years.

The documents not only confirmed the reality of UFOs and gave detailed descriptions of them, they also gave researchers access to numerous reports from credible witnesses – scientists, military personnel and law enforcement officers. Some of the documents released originated from other agencies. This confirmed that every other US agency had also been studying the UFO phenomenon and that the military had been involved in UFO research even before 1947.

Bolstered by this success, Gersten formed Citizens Against UFO Secrecy (CAUS), an organisation dedicated to breaking down the wall of secrecy surrounding the UFO phenomenon. Its aim is to force the government to come clean on what it knows about contact with extraterrestrial intelligence, and it believes that the public has the absolute and unconditional right to know.

In the early 1980s, Gersten continued his legal assault on the US intelligence community, taking the National Security Agency to court after the NSA refused an FOIA request for UFO-related documents that CAUS knew they had in their possession. In court, the judge asked the NSA's attorney how many documents had surfaced when they had processed the CAUS's FOIA request. He was told that it was classified information. Gersten told the judge that the CIA had told him that the NSA had at least eighteen documents. The judge then insisted that the NSA come up with a figure. The agency finally admitted that there were 135. But that was as far as it went. The NSA invoked the National Security Exemption, one of twelve exemption clauses built into the FOIA. To argue their exemption, the NSA used a twenty-one-page affidavit that was itself classified, and the case was dismissed.

Although Gersten was unsuccessful in obtaining the UFO documents, he did succeed in getting the NSA to admit that they held them. He took the appeal to the Supreme Court and, when it was dismissed, it made headline news. Even though he did not get the documents, he had succeeded in drawing great attention to the issue of UFO secrecy and highlighted the US Supreme Court's role in this cover-up. In further court actions, Gersten succeed in forcing the release of a heavily censored version of the NSA exemption affidavit and, in due course, most of the documents they withheld have been released.

Gersten is not optimistic about the efforts of various organisations – such as Dr Steven Greer's Center for the Study of Extraterrestrial Intelligence – to get the US Congress to hold open hearings on the subject of UFOs. He says that the idea of open hearings is inherently ridiculous because any discussion of UFOs involves a discussion of advanced technology. This is an area that the military keeps secret by invoking national security, while the corporations protect their developments by using patents. The elected officials of Congress are always up for re-election – every two years for Representatives and six years for Senators. They need money and are always vulnerable to the demands of special interests.

Getting Congress to grant immunity to people who may have to break secrecy oaths to testify would not help. Gersten points out the problems: 'Let's say you have a general who wants to testify in a Congressional hearing even though he is sworn to secrecy. He will naturally expect Congress to grant him immunity. However, the military will then question Congress's right to grant immunity and they would then have to fight it out in the courts, which could take years.'

Gersten finds it more effective to work through CAUS, which makes it possible for him to protect the privacy of any informant, through client–attorney privilege, but at the same time get the information out.

He used the Freedom of Information Act to try to pressurise the US Army into releasing documents relating to statements made by Colonel Philip J. Corso in his book, *The Day After Roswell*. Corso was willing to testify that he had seen the bodies of dead aliens in 1947 and that he had read alien autopsy reports in 1961. Gersten was ready to take the issue to court, so he filed an FOIA request with the US Army for the release of any documents they may have had supporting Corso's claims. The Army claimed it could find no documents and Gersten took them to court. But Corso died and, on 26 April 1999, the case was dismissed. Gersten decided not to take that matter any further. Instead he filed a suit against the Department of Defense over Flying Triangles, in an attempt to find out what these mysterious craft actually are. While Gersten concedes that some of the sighting reports clearly describe advanced US experimental aircraft such as the TR-3B, which researcher Ed Fouche claims was built at Area 51, many of the reports could not possibly be the TR-3B. People have seen triangular craft that are half-a-mile wide. Some are seen at treetop level and over populated areas, shining beams of light on the ground. Witnesses also report seeing orb-shaped lights detach from these craft, fly around and re-attach. None of this can be explained in terms of advanced military technology.

Gersten sued the US government for damages after Betty Cash, Vickie Landrum and her grandson were abducted in Texas on the night of 29 December 1980. Gersten argued that as the UFO concerned was escorted by twenty Chinook helicopters it must have been part of a military operation. The case was dismissed on the grounds that the government denied all knowledge of the UFO and Gersten could not prove that it belonged to them.

Gersten is also bringing an unprecedented FOIA lawsuit against the CIA, the FBI and Department of Defense on the grounds that alien abduction can be viewed legally as a form of invasion. Article 4, section 4 of the US Constitution requires that the Federal Government protect the individual states against invasion, a provision that was enacted to persuade the original colonies to abandon their independent militias and join the Union. However, the Federal government are plainly failing in their duty to protect citizens of the States if those citizens are being abducted.

CAUS and Gersten have even more ambitious plans. As it is unlikely that the President is likely to open up all the files on UFOs in the foreseeable future, they want to find out for themselves. They are planning a privately funded mission to the Moon, to send back pictures from the Sinu Medi regions where some UFOlogists have locateed alien structures. Using existing technology, they estimate that their 'Project Destination Moon' would cost $12 million – small change to the likes of Bill Gates and Ted Turner.

'Think of all the money sponsors would make from the publicity if they funded the first civilian mission to the Moon, especially if alien artefacts were discovered,' says the ever-optimistic Gersten. 'The space programme is in the hands of the government and the military. We are all like virtual prisoners on this planet. This is a project that is just waiting to happen.'

Derrel Sims

Alien implant expert Derrel Sims is a former CIA operative and got involved in UFO research after being abducted himself. He has conscious recollections of multiple abductions between the ages of three and seventeen. He started researching in this field at the age of sixteen and has been at it for more than twenty-seven years. After leaving the world of covert intelligence, he rose to become chief of investigation for the Houston-based Fund for Interactive Research and Space Technology. There he concentrated on collecting physical evidence, as he believes that this is the best way to prove that UFOs and alien abductions actually exist.

He has investigated hundreds of cases of alien implants, some of which have been inside the body for up to forty-one years. Despite being foreign bodies, they trigger no inflammatory response. He says that the devices found are 'meteoric' in origin. Although some labs have said that this is impossible, 'double blind' tests had proved this to be the case.

Dr Roger Leir

For years, people doubted the reality of alien abductions. This was largely because abductees had no physical evidence to back their stories. One man changed all that – Dr Roger Leir. A podiatrist from south California, he was the first doctor surgically to remove an alien implant. Until his first operation in August 1995, they had been seen only on X-rays and CAT scans.

Leir had a long interest in UFOs and was a long-standing member of the Mutual UFO Network, where he gained an investigator's certificate. As an investigator, he attended a UFO conference in Los Angeles in June 1995, when he met Derrel Sims. Sims showed Leir a number of X-rays. One of them showed a foreign object in the big toe of an abductee. Leir was sceptical, but Derrel produced the abductee's medical records, which showed that she had never had surgery on her foot. Leir offered to remove it and this led to a series of operations on abductees.

He selects candidates for surgery by strict criteria, which were developed when Leir was working at the National Institute for

Discovery Science. Anyone undergoing surgery had to be a suspected abductee – they had to have experienced missing time or, at
the very least, seen a UFO. They had to fill out a form that determined how deeply they were involved in the abduction phenomenon. They also had to have an object in their body that showed up
on an X-ray, CAT scan or MRI.

Some of Leir's patients would have a conscious memory of the
object being implanted into their bodies during the abduction. But,
more often, implants are discovered by accident. Some abductees
find unusual lumps and scars that have suddenly appeared and go
to their doctors to get them X-rayed. In one case, an implant was
discovered during treatment following a car crash.

All Leir's patients are given a psychological examination before
and after the implant is removed. Some of them experience a new-
found sense of freedom after surgery. One abductee went straight
back to her family, saying she wanted nothing more to do with
UFOs.

Leir has, so far, operated on eight individuals and removed a
total of nine objects. Seven of them seem to be of extraterrestrial
origin. Five were coated in a dark grey shiny membrane that was
impossible to cut through even with a brand new surgical blade.
One was T-shaped. Another three were greyish-white balls that
were attached to an abnormal area of the skin. Leir found that
patients would react violently if the object was touched and often
suffered pain in that area in the week before the implant was surgically removed.

During surgery, Leir discovered that there was no inflammatory
response in the flesh around the implant. He found this surprising as
any foreign object introduced into the body usually causes an
inflammatory response. In this case, there was no rejection. He also
found that the surrounding tissue also contained large numbers of
'proprioceptors'. These are specialised nerve cells usually found in
sensitive areas, such the finger tips, which sense temperature,
pressure and touch. There was no medical reason for them to be
found where he found them, clustered around the implant. In two
cases, Leir found 'scoop mark' lesions above the implants. In each

case, Leir found that the tissue there suffered from a condition called 'solar elastosis'. This is caused by exposure to ultraviolet light, but it could not have been due to sunburn as only a tiny area was affected.

Leir found that the membrane surrounding the implants was composed of the protein coagulum, hemosiderin granules – an iron pigment – and keratin. All these three substances are found naturally in the body. However, a search of the medical literature revealed that they had never been found together in combination before.

The implants themselves would fluoresce under ultraviolet light – usually green, but sometimes other colours. In one case, Leir found that an abductee had a pink stain on the palm of her hand. It could be removed temporarily, but would seep back under the skin. Derrel Sims uses this fluorescent staining, which cannot be removed by washing, to detect implants. Leir believes that it is caused by a substance given off by the implant to prevent rejection.

A wide range of tests have been carried out on the implants Leir has removed. They are submitted to routine pathology tests to see if they are human in origin. When that draws a blank, they are sent for metallurgical testing and they have been examined under optical microscopes and electron microscopes, and analysed using X-ray diffraction techniques that tell which elements they are made of.

When the T-shaped implant that Leir had removed from one patient was magnified one thousand times under an electron microscope, a tiny fishhook could be seen on one end of the crossbar of the T, which Leir believes anchored the implant to the flesh. The other end was rounded off like the nose of a bullet, while in the middle there was a tiny hole into which the shaft of the T fitted perfectly. One of the rods had a carbon core, which made it electrically conductive. The other had an iron core, which was magnetic. An attractive force between them made them cling together. The shaft was encircled by a band of silicate crystals. Bob Beckworth, an electrical engineer who works with Leir, likened this to an old-fashioned crystal set, where a quartz crystal and a copper wire were used to pick up a radio signal.

Specimens were sent to some of the most prestigious laboratories in North America – Los Alamos National Laboratories, New Mexico Tech and Toronto University, among others. The samples were found to contain rare elements in the same isotopic ratios that are found in meteorites. When the labs were told that the specimens had been removed from body tissue, they did not believe it. For Leir, this is the smoking gun.

When you mine an element on Earth, the ratio of the various radioactive isotopes it contains always falls within a certain range. If you mine uranium, for example, it will always contain a certain ratio of uranium 234, 235 and 236. This will be roughly the same anywhere on Earth. But rock samples from the moon or meteorites contain completely different isotopic ratios. The isotopic ratios in the implants showed clearly that they were not of earthly origin.

Leir is not sure what the implants are for. They could be transponders or locating devices that enable alien abductors to track those they have abducted. They might be designed to modify behaviour – some abductees exhibit unexplained compulsive behaviour. They might detect chemical changes in the body, caused by pollution. Or they might be used to detect genetic changes in the body.

'If researchers such as Zachariah Sitchen are correct,' says Leir, 'and the human race is a genetically altered species, then it's possible that this genetic manipulation may still be going on and is something "they" wish to monitor closely.'

But what ever the implants are for, it is quite clear that they are extraterrestrial in origin. As Leir points out, if you find people who have been abducted by aliens and then find implants in them that have an isotopic ratio not found this planet, what other sane conclusion can you draw?

Tony Dodd

Ex-Sergeant Tony Dodd became interested in UFOs after having an encounter with one himself in 1978, when he was a police officer in North Yorkshire, England. He saw an object hovering about a hundred feet away. It had a domed top with four doors it. There were flashing lights around the sides, and three large spheres protruding from the underside. The whole structure was glowing bright white and it was silent. Dodd was sure this strange object was homing in on him, though it eventually floated off and landed nearby.

After he reported his sighting, his superiors told him not to talk to the press. This was standard procedure in the police.

Since then, he has seen seventy or eighty UFOs. Some of them are simply balls of light, anything from a couple of feet to thirty feet across. However, they seemed to contain some kind of mechanical device. He could often see a small, red pulse of light inside them, which created the aura of light. He has received hundreds of reports of these balls of light, which apparently fly in formation. That must mean they have intelligent controls, he reasons.

After retiring from the police force, Dodd took the opportunity to speak out. He devoted himself to UFO research full-time and became Director of Investigative Services for Quest International, one of the world's leading UFO societies, and he oversees the publication of their high influential *UFO Magazine*. For part of his time in the police, he was a detective and he uses police investigation techniques on UFO cases. His police background has taught him which lines of enquiry to pursue and how to encourage witnesses to come forward and talk. It has also given him contacts in intelligence and the military. This is not always an advantage. Dodd's mail is tampered with, even the registered packages that turn up. And the CIA have threatened to kill him, though he remains stoically unintimidated.

Dodd is the foremost expert on animal mutilations in the UK and believes the government know all about it. He also believes that elite forces in America and Britain had adopted a hostile attitude towards a certain type of alien because the aliens out there do not resemble us very closely. Aliens, he points out, do not necessarily have two legs and two arms. Indeed, in human eyes some are quite grotesque. This is the reason the aliens are abducting people and creating hybrids. The aliens, apparently feel the same way about us. When people are abducted, they are treated the way we treat animals on game reserves.

Abductions are never one-off incidents, he says. Dodd has never come across a victim who has been abducted in childhood and never abducted again. Once it has happened, it tends to occur throughout the victim's life. Dodd believes that abductees are being conditioned until they reach puberty. After that the visitors start taking sperm and eggs. Part of the alien's agenda, Dodd believes, is a genetic experiment to create human–alien hybrids. He has investigated cases where aliens have impregnated female abductees. The conception is not natural. It is performed with a needle that it inserted through the navel. Human babies can be conceived using similar methods, but our medical profession is years behind. Three months into the pregnancy, the abductee is picked up again and the foetus is taken from the womb. The resulting 'star children' have thin limbs, large heads and alien eyes and faces, though they have hair on their heads and small human noses.

One woman he knows has been impregnated twice and both times the aliens have taken the baby. When the woman was three months pregnant, she was out walking her dog and a strange light appeared in the sky. She knew they had come to take her baby. She also saw jars containing embryos, which were suspended in liquid, as if in an artificial womb. These jars were all around the walls of the room she was in.

In many of the cases that Dodd has investigated, the abductees seem to have a sixth sense. They get a feeling when they know the abduction is about to take place. However, people generally do not know that they have been abducted. The clue is when they know things that they would not normally know about.

He uses lie detectors in his investigations. But he also uses his knowledge of the subject and his police background to sniff out the hoaxers. He also uses hypnosis and always employs the same hypnotist. This is because the man does nothing more than put the subject under hypnosis. Dodd himself asks all the questions. This is vital because he does not want the witnesses to be led or have them given guidance or pointers.

In abduction cases, Dodd also looks for physical evidence. Some abductees have strange marks on their bodies. In one case he investigated, a woman saw strange balls of light in her bedroom at night, and she had an inexplicable burn mark on her arm. The woman had contacted him after he had made radio broadcast about alien abductions and, although many of the things he had mentioned had happened to her, she wanted to be reassured that she had not been abducted.

He has also come across a case where an abductee set off a camera flash near an alien implant in his head. Something under his skin glowed green. It was about a quarter of an inch wide, but it did not seem to cause the man any pain.

On several occasions, Dodd has had a person under hypnosis who has ended up speaking as somebody else – one of the aliens, Dodd believes. When he asked them what right they had to abduct people, the alien voice replied: 'We have every right to do this, you do not understand the nature of things.' Dodd concluded that he was talking to a highly intelligent being.

Dodd has tried to develop this as a method of communication with the alien race and has come to believe that extra-terrestrial beings are involved in a collect-and-analyse experiment to study the human race. He is in regular communication with them, but they only divulge things piece by piece. When he gets impatient, they tell him that they have to take things slowly because the human race is not able to handle the truth. We have to be educated as if we were in infant school. Dodd finds this very spiritual.

This is why they are not communicating with all of us. We are not ready for the knowledge they possess. That is why Dodd himself is here. His role is to disseminate information, to learn from the aliens and to give what he knows out to humankind. His alien contacts have told him that he is some form of teacher. Apparently this was decided before he arrived on Earth as a child and it is why they are making contact with him. They have explained humankind's place in the universe and have told him that we are immortal spirits that go on and on.

'Every flower has its seed and every creature its destiny,' Dodd has been told. 'Weep not for those who have fulfilled their earthly obligation, but be happy that they have escaped that charge of material suffering. As the flower dies, the seed is born and so shall it be for all things.'

Dodd's contact with the aliens has religious aspects. He believes that they are a higher force and that they are responsible for us being here.

A.J. Gevaerd

A. J. Gevaerd is Brazil's leading UFOlogist, editor of the country's only UFO publication, *UFO*, and the director of the Brazilian Centre for Flying Saucer Research, the largest organisation of its kind in the country. He came to international attention in 1996,through his investigation of the famous Varginha case, where two extraterrestrials were captured after their spacecraft crashed in southern Brazil.

According to Gevaerd, there were numerous UFO sightings in the first few weeks of 1996. On the night of 19 January, two people reported seeing a spacecraft which had difficulty flying. At around 7:30 a.m. on the morning of 20 January, a number of people in the town of Varginha reported spotting a humanoid creature around. It had red eyes, a reddish-brown coloured skin and three small bumps on its head. Frightened residents called the Fire Department. They located the creature in an area called Jardim Andere and called the Brazilian army. By 10:30 a.m., army personnel and firemen had managed to net the creature and placed it in a crate. They then took it to the School of the Sergeant of Arms in the nearby town of Tres Coracoes.

Gevaerd discovered that a second extraterrestrial was found later that day. Three girls saw another creature cowering by a wall not far from where the first one had been captured. They told Gevaerd that it had a large head, brown skin, thick veins on its upper body and three protuberances on its head that looked like horns. At 8:30 p.m., a military vehicle with two policemen in it almost drove over a creature Gevaerd believes was the same as the one seen by the girls. One of the officers jumped out of the truck and grabbed it with his bare hands. He held it in his lap until they reached a nearby medical facility. Gevaerd discover that the creature was later transferred to the Humanitas Hospital in Varginha. The capture of the second creature occurred on a Saturday night when everyone was out on the streets. Many people saw the commotion and military trucks pulling up. In all, Gevaerd and his fellow researchers have interviewed over forty witnesses who saw the authorities capture the two creatures.

The aliens' UFO was first detected by an American satellite and the US informed the Brazilian military as part of an agreement between the two nations. So Brazilian radar was on full alert when the craft entered Brazilian airspace and it tracked the craft until it crashed into the state of Minas Gerais. Gevaerd has proof that both the US and the Brazilian government knew immediately that a UFO had crashed and knew roughly its location. Gevaerd tried to get details but there was a complete clamp down in the military. He believes that both extraterrestrials survived the crash, but died within a few hours of capture. The crash seems to have left them badly injured. The crash had occurred at around 3 a.m. When people saw them a few hours later, they were on their last legs.

'It could have been due to the crash,' says Gevaerd. 'Or perhaps the environment was not suitable.'

Gevaerd believes that the US was involved from the start. He knows the creatures were later moved to the Hospital of Clinics at the University of Campinas. There were examined by a team of doctors, headed by Brazil's leading forensic scientist, Dr Furtunato Badan Palhares. In all, fifteen masked doctors examined the creatures' bodies, and seven of the team were non-Brazilians – probably US scientists. Gevaerd also thinks that the bodies were shipped to the US. A special US transport plane arrived on 26 January at Campinas, and he thinks that the bodies were taken to an Air Force base in North America.

'Everything indicates US involvement,' says Gevaerd. 'Our government does what it's told to do by the US. They co-operate with the US in return for favours.'

Since the Varginha incident, Gevaerd has consolidated his reputation by his investigation of 'Operation Saucer'. This began in 1977 when hundreds of UFO sightings came from an area along the Amazon river. Many people said they had been attacked by beams of light. Later many of them suffered symptoms of anaemia, although it is not clear whether this was due to loss of blood or to receiving a discharge from a UFO. The state authorities sent in teams of doctors, but they were attacked too. Eventually, the central government took the problem seriously, and, in September 1977, a team of twelve men from the Brazilian Air Force were sent to the area to investigate. They collected reports from over three thousand people who had seen UFOs and had been attacked by balls of light. This inquiry was called 'Operation Saucer' and was headed by Colonel Uyrange Hollanda, who told his story to Gevaerd in 1987, shortly before committing suicide.

The Operation Saucer team were ordered to talk to witnesses, document the evidence and get photographs – they took five hundred photographs of the UFOs in all. Hollanda's team were also ordered to see if they could make contact with the aliens and ask them why they had come. Although he got no direct answer to this question, Hollanda believed that the aliens were here to collect genetic material. Attacks usually took place when victims were alone and isolated. They would see a ball of light moving towards them. It would give them an electric shock, which would put them to sleep for several hours. When they regained consciousness, they would find small scars on their bodies, which Hollanda believed was caused by the extraction of tissue samples. But the damage was not just physical. Many victims suffered trauma and many were terrified. One fisherman who was attacked repeatedly was so terrified that he broke a leg while fleeing, Gevaerd says, but continued running despite his injury.

Hollanda reported seeing the craft associated with the attacks. They were sleek and teardrop-shaped with a large transparent area at the front, like a helicopter canopy, he told Gevaerd. On occasions, alien figures could be seen moving around inside. Towards the end of their investigations, short, humanoid, Grey aliens were regularly seen by the team. According to Gevaerd, the team's presence seemed to attract the interest of the extraterrestrials. Hollanda told Gevaerd that the aliens seemed to know everything the team did before they did it. For instance, if they decided to go up river, they would find the aliens waiting when they got there. Team members felt as though they were being observed. Eventually, the military team themselves fell victim to attacks. All members of the team were abducted. Hollanda himself was subjected to multiple abductions, during which he was examined both physically and psychologically by the aliens. He also told Gevaerd that he had acquired paranormal abilities as a result of his contacts.

However, these abductions caused Hollanda to lose his emotional stability. When Gevaerd interviewed him in July 1987, he broke down and wept. When he described his contact with the aliens he was obviously under great strain and was still plagued by strange phenomena years after he left the Amazon. He committed suicide two days before the first of a series of sessions of regressional hypnosis Gevaerd had arranged for him, thinking this might help.

Operation Saucer concluded that there was no doubt that the UFOs were responsible for the attacks. It also found that people were being abducted; some did not return. Gevaerd does not know why these abductions were happening, or why the aliens had such a special interest in the natives of the Amazon – although it is possible they conducted their experiments in this area because the people were isolated, living far from any protection.

Gevaerd finds the phenomenon of abduction a big puzzle. He has investigated cases where abductees have acquired paranormal abilities, including telepathic and healing powers, as a result. One case that Gevaerd investigated was that of Vera Lucia Guimaraes Borges, who was abducted in the 1960s when she was a teenager. She was living in the house of her grandmother in Valencia, near Rio de Janeiro, when she was woken one night by a noise and was lured into the kitchen. There she was confronted by a ball of light, which hovered in front of her. She promptly fainted. After this incident, Borges acquired remarkable paranormal powers, including the ability to diagnose a patient's illness by simply thinking about them. Under regressional hypnosis, she discovered that she had been abducted by two aliens – one male and one female in appearance – who had subjected her to a medical examination.

Doctors were called in by Gevaerd to test her diagnostic skills. She was 99 per cent accurate. One of the doctors was so impressed that he used her as a consultant. In one case, she told him that a young male patient had been bitten by a poisonous creature and told him which antidote to use.

'I know of many cases where abductees have acquired paranormal abilities,' says Gevaerd. 'Although abductions appear to have no obvious benefits, there are plenty of cases that illustrate we are visited by ETs who can help us do special things.'

However, Hollanda certainly did not benefit from his abduction, and other abductees gain nothing and end up traumatised. Although there are a lot of dedicated UFO researchers in Brazil, only a few are investigating abductions. As a result, Gevaerd is collaborating with the North American alien abduction experts Budd Hopkins and Dr John Mack, who he hopes will teach Brazilian investigators how to do abduction research.

'There is so much new data here that has not yet been seized upon by the media,' says Gevaerd. He believes that it could be the clue to an enigma. 'I'm convinced humanity, in a number of different forms, is spread out all over the universe. We are just a tiny fraction of what exists.'